What your travel agent may NOT tell you about Bora Bora

The secrets to saving

in Bora Bora

By Gloria Altus & Melinda Altus-Richardson

Visit http://www.boraboraislandguide.com for more information.

Table of Contents

How to make your dream Bora Bora vacation reality...

With the average holiday in Bora Bora costing over $10,000 it's no ordinary vacation! Tahiti is one of the most remote island groups in the world which is why it has remained pristine and exclusive. Everything...from getting here, to staying and eating here...costs.

Many people claim that Bora Bora is expensive, but don't let those nay sayers scare you away from making a visit a reality. While things in Tahiti might cost more than at home or in cheap, popular, vacation places like Mexico or Bali, you'll find the cost relative to other special island destinations.

While this book is about how to save money, this book is about an *extraordinary* destination. So we also intend talking about what is actually worth spending on, if you can.

Throughout, we will show you, how much you can save during an average weeks' vacation by applying the tips we share. You will find this at the end of each section under *SAVINGS*.

We appreciate that we're speaking to a broad audience, which has quite different expectations about what a vacation should be. We know you are accustomed to different levels of luxury (or require none at all)! We ourselves have done it *all* ways because we were inspired by distant lands in our youth, so began traveling with small purses and gradually were able to explore with bank balances that cushioned us in comfort and costlier adventures.

There's one common thread. You all want to see the world's most admired island at the best possible price which also fits into your budget. So we share how to get a good deal and do it at every level, and readers can take the nuggets applicable to them.

Things to Know Before You Go:

Perhaps you've been on an island holiday before. But if you haven't been to Bora Bora, you can't imagine the treat you are in for! Forget all your preconceived ideas about what an island vacation is and get ready to take in all the info you need to plan and book the perfect getaway.

Tahiti is Not Hawaii

There is no Walmart, Costco or Trader Joe's way out here. Almost everything is imported from Europe which means that basic, everyday items cost more. Use our "what to pack list" to make sure that you take everything you will need, for the season in which you go.

English is a second language for almost everyone living in Tahiti. It's actually the third language of islanders who switch from Polynesian at home to French in school and the workplace. With the advent of tourism in recent times some are learning English to communicate with clients at work. Don't expect *everyone* to speak English, and do learn to pronounce the few Polynesian greetings we share below.

Tahiti is Not Mexico

Many folk ask how they can have an all-inclusive Bora Bora vacation, thinking it will save money. But Tahiti is *not* an all-inclusive destination in the way Mexico or the Caribbean are. You will read in the eating section why we don't usually recommend you pay an inclusive price that covers full board at your resort.

An issue you won't have to think about in Tahiti is safety. There's no drug cartels or kidnappings out here! The islanders live peacefully on "island time", and won't even disturb the reverie to go fishing, unless they need to. Of course, it's still sensible to be careful with your loose valuables, and also a bicycle, if you decide to save money by following our self-drive

Circle Island Tour.

There is no cheap labor or vast land for farming, out on these scattered islands, either, so naturally food will cost more than at resorts which have been especially built in places where they cash in on those. So we tell you how to eat like the locals.

Tahiti is Not the Caribbean

You will be surprised by how quiet the famous white sand beaches are. (I always wonder where everyone else is!) No one will interrupt your relaxation, attempting to badger you into buying sunglasses, bags or hats; or try to make you feel guilty if you say no. There's no need to spend on unintended purchases or cultivate a do-not-disturb face on these islands. And when you approach a vendor or stall that's been set up (and there aren't many) you will be treated with dignity. Unlike in the Caribbean, you can simply *relax* in Tahiti and not feel forced into purchasing goods by harassment on the beach or in markets. We didn't appreciate how peaceful Tahiti beaches truly are until we cruised the Caribbean and were frequently confronted by wandering salesmen.

Tahiti is Not Bali

Bali is known for its cheap flights, cheap hotel accommodation, and cheap cost of living. In Bali people have to work for next to nothing. You can get a villa complete with servant to cook meals, and indulge in a cheap massage (in public) on the beach every day.

The scene in Tahiti is entirely different. People don't go there to get drunk and they don't hire out villas and over-fill them with partying friends. There are no drunken Australians to spoil the romance in Tahiti! The distance and cost to get there helps keep the crowds down.

In Tahiti people are paid fair wages and everyone's choice of lifestyle and religion is accepted. The fact that there is no terrorism or violence caused by conflicts in religion makes it one of the safest regions in the world right now.

Tahiti is Not Thailand

Bora Bora has only 3 sleepy villages. There's no Sin City with red light brothels in this beachside haven. You won't have to hurry past any suspicious looking X-rated premises, or fend off lady-boys and shady characters offering massages with happy endings.

The military isn't in charge. It's an extremely stable country governed by French principles and standards. It's a comfort knowing that there's access to world class health care, should it be needed. Many tourists visiting Asia have scooter injuries requiring them to be urgently flown back home for hospitalization. The traffic in Thailand is chaotic and dangerous. There's masses of scooters, tuk tuks, and buses. Contrast that with Bora Bora and its one scenic road, quietly circling the island. But in Tahiti you will still get the luscious tropical fruit for a nice price!

Tahiti is Not the Mediterranean

You don't have to pay to visit a beach in Tahiti. Some are classified 'private' because they are owned by folk living nearby. There are also plenty of public ones to freely enjoy. The fabulous French Polynesian beaches are spacious and relaxing. Unlike Europe, there's no need to book for a tiny space with a sun chair and umbrella where you are allowed to sit for a specified length of time (with the meter running).

You won't have to shoo away pushy hawkers trying to sell you a massage, bag, or pair of sunglasses either. Tahitians are gentle people who wait for folk to come and buy their pretty traditional crafts from a stall.

There are no hard or hot pebbles on Tahiti beaches. All beaches have sand, not stones. Due to past volcanic activity, there are wondrous variations in sand colors. You can see extraordinary black-sand Lafayette Beach in front of the Pearl Beach Resort on Tahiti's main island, and another, smaller one, fronting the Sofitel Moorea Ia Ora Beach Resort on

Moorea.

Out in the atolls there are unusual pink sand beaches...quietly waiting to be discovered. You'll read how to fly to several islands while only paying a few dollars more than the cost of Bora Bora flights.

Bora Bora's famous *Matira* is voted most beautiful beach in the world. You can meet locals and travelers from anywhere in the world on this *free* 2 mile stretch of white sand. It's amazing how the largest part is bare on any day of the year, except one! Each November the inter-island Havaki Nui canoe race ends here, and there are so many people celebrating that the water turns brown from the sand being stirred up.

In Europe there are only a few places where you can actually *stay on* a beach! In Bora Bora the primary feature of every resort is its pinch-me...am I awake?...dreamy setting, which offers complimentary use (anywhere, anytime) of its exquisite private beach and watercraft.

Planning and Booking

The most important actions we want you to take from this section are to:
- Start planning *early;*
- Decide what type of stay is right for you; and
- Calculate the best pricing you can find yourself and/or
- Check what a *specialist Tahiti travel agent* can offer for a package.

When to Go?

Hotel rates and flight prices are determined by 3 seasons in Bora Bora: low season, high season and shoulder season. If you want to save money on the largest expenditures of your trip - your hotel and flight - simply avoid traveling in high season, which is in June, July and August. This also means you will avoid the crowds. (Not that Bora Bora ever gets hoards of people; like the Mediterranean, the Caribbean, or the main islands of Hawaii!)

How Much Do You Need to spend?

While our prime purpose is to point out every smart way to save money on your trip, there are some things that *must* be experienced on this unique adventure. Year after year Bora Bora is voted (by travelers) as the number one island in the world to holiday on. We provide information to help you decide; where to direct your funds, what is worth paying a little extra for, and what you can skimp on. We love this water world and we want you to have a wonderful time. If something is worth the money, we will tell you. And if we know ways you can save on an alternative, we will tell you!

How Long to Go For?

Every night in Tahiti is going to cost money. (Unless you know the credit card to have!) A five-day trip, which you can buy an all-year-round discount flight for, allows you to experience Bora Bora. However, only use that option if budget or time constraints are too tight to stay longer. We suggest that once you fly there, stay at least a week. There are so many beautiful islands, spread over an area as large as Europe, that you could come here for a few months and not see everything. Make your trip as long as you can. Use some of the accommodation saving tips in the next chapter to help you stay longer. Consider that once you fly here, the cost per day for your vacation will decrease with every extra day you stay.

To Travel Agent or Not to Travel Agent?

Thanks to the internet, there are many travel savvy people who book their entire vacation online. You're probably one of those people, which is why you found your way to our site, and invested in this eBook. We've been those people too. It's easy to self-book for many places in the world where rooms are sold en-mass to highly trafficked places.

But planning a trip to French Polynesia isn't as simple as snapping up a hotel and flight for a bargain price. It took us several trips to know *what there is to know* about all the choices! In this eBook we're sharing the most valuable gems.

Those wishing to stay at the lower and mid-range levels of accommodation will benefit immensely from our tips. It's knowledge that will empower you to make wise decisions *and* save money on all aspects of a vacation in Bora Bora. When you know what you want, calculate the costing at the best prices you find. You may have found the best prices and it's reassuring to know that. Run your requirements past an agent to make a comparison.

Not just any travel agent though. The world offers such a kaleidoscope of choices that a regular agent simply cannot know enough about "Everywhere". Bora Bora is a holiday destination unlike any other!

Most Bora Bora hotels sell with individual agreements, rather than the fixed prices that are standardly used elsewhere. If the agent approaches the task in the same way they plan a trip to any other destination, you won't get the best deal possible.

Utilizing a *destination specialist* has superb advantages. They understand the uniqueness of the world's most beautiful island. They visit the resorts regularly and have the influence to negotiate great prices. Yes, a dedicated Tahiti travel agent can be your guardian angel who ensures every detail is perfect. But choose one who speaks fluent English, so all communications are clear. There is one agent we choose to work with, you can follow the link and receive a quote from them in the Resources section of this book.

Choosing to Stay 4 or 5 Star?

If you're choosing to stay four or five star, travel specialists are usually able to include free upgrades, and score you extras, at no additional cost. There's more room for price movement. If you're planning a wedding or a honeymoon, they can also arrange some lovely surprises with your resort. So combine our guide with booking your much-anticipated vacation through an experienced Tahiti destination specialist and you will enjoy many extra benefits, while also saving money with almost every decision you make.

There is only one agent which we have personal experience with, and can recommend. We liaise with a boutique agency which organizes packages at the four and five-star level. They only book resorts which their clients have consistently reported good results from staying at. If you are seeking luxury accommodation they offer *wholesale-like prices* that are simply the best to be found. By booking through them, you can get deals not offered to the general public or found on the internet.

Their outstanding service goes far beyond best prices. They know this isn't any ordinary trip and will help you plan a tailor-made, bespoke vacation. Their attention to detail extends to while you're lying on a beach in Bora Bora. You'll be given a mobile phone number (in the same time zone) to call if anything isn't going quite right (and they also speak fluent French). You just enjoy the ride! Find contact details in the Resources section at the end.

All Things Money

Although Tahiti is a distant paradise, the main islands that are visited by tourists, the Society Islands, are generally well connected to the world. In these more populated isles, where Bora Bora lies, credit cards are accepted at supermarkets, most restaurants, hotels, and for tours. Plus you will find an ATM and bank on most of these islands. To enjoy some of the unusual experiences, and utilize spontaneous opportunities to save dollars, you will want to have some Pacific Francs (CFP) on hand.

How to Save Money with Every Transaction:

Get a Card with No International Transaction Fees
Currency conversion rates are usually best with credit card use or ATM withdrawals. You can use a Visa or Mastercard at most places in Bora Bora. There are only a few places that don't accept credit cards. Make sure you have a credit card that *does not charge international transaction fees*. They add up to a sum worth saving!
Savings: $100+ in international fees

Be Selective in Sourcing CFP Cash
You'll get a better exchange rate converting money either before you travel, or at the airport when you arrive in Papeete, than exchanging at your hotel. Although many flights arrive at night there's a convenient 24-hour ATM service available at Faa'a International Airport. Find it on the left as you leave the building. Source a few hundred dollars' worth of U.S. in local Pacific Francs. Some smaller stores and vendors don't take credit cards and you will want to have cash handy to purchase the best bargains. Avoid converting money at hotels, but keep in mind that it's possible if absolutely necessary.

A good option is to contact a bank in your hometown a couple of weeks before your trip and tell them the amount of French Pacific Francs (CFP) you require. It may take a few days for the bank to get the money in, before you can pick it up. Some banks exchange rate fee is only a few dollars

(rather than a percentage) no matter how much you exchange. Be warned that the worst exchange rate will be at LAX airport.
Savings: at least $20+ in your pocket from a better exchange rate (depending on your level of spending)

Be aware: If you have to exchange money at a bank on Bora Bora, make sure you have your passport with you.

Use a Debit Card with No Withdrawal Fee

An ATM will give you a better conversion rate than any other place of exchange. I hold a Citibank debit card because I can use it in ATMs overseas and not be charged a withdrawal fee. The currency conversion rate is better than exchanging actual money. Make sure you check your card's fee beforehand, or you could be charged an extra $5 fee on each withdrawal.

Factor in that getting cash from ATM's in Tahiti can be unreliable. Plan ahead. Keep account of how much you have in your purse and organize more before you use it all up. Sometimes ATMs around Tahiti don't spit out money. I once had the *third-try-lucky* experience, after being unable to source cash at two previous banks. I thought my bank had abandoned me! Don't assume that your card is at fault. Some overseas banks don't seem to be recognized by some Tahiti banks. Also keep in mind that ATMs may run out of cash, especially on weekends, and each ATM in Tahiti can vary the amount they will allow you to withdraw.
Savings: $100+ in transaction fees

Avoid Using $US Notes

US currency *may* be accepted as direct payment in hotels, restaurants and large shops, but you will receive a poor rate of exchange. Although some places allow payment in US dollars, resist the urge of ease as you will pay extra! For example, an item could be priced at 4000 CFP or 40 USD. As 4000 CFP is worth about 36 USD you will be overpaying if you use USD instead of CFP. One exception is if you are cruising across the pacific and your itinerary has a day in Bora Bora, don't bother about getting CPF, use USD.

Savings: $50+ if you buy sundries and souvenirs with CFP

Always Have Local Currency on You

Most places that take credit cards have a rather high minimum spend. For example, the little convenience store by the Intercontinental Le Moana has a minimum spend of 2000 CFP (about USD$18). You definitely want to have cash on hand so you are not forced to spend more than intended. Keep a few dollars handy in local cash for a bottle of water or a roadside snack.

Don't miss out on any opportunities! Once we were traveling along the Circle Island Road and had no cash in our purse. There was a table with large bowls of freshly picked mangoes, for just $2 a bowl, set up by the roadside. (Fruit falls of trees in the wild.) But we couldn't buy any. You need cash in your pocket for when you stumble upon the best bargains in Bora Bora. If you intend hanging out at your resort, basking on a sun lounge during your entire vacation, you will not need CFP currency.

Savings: $20+
Avoiding missed opportunities: priceless!

Where to Find an ATM in Bora Bora

Most ATM's in Bora Bora are located in Vaitape, the main town. There is an ATM at the post office, one at Banque de Tahiti, and two at Banque Socredo.

Although the airport has an ATM, this is on a separate island so can only be used when arriving or leaving Bora Bora. If you're staying on a motu, either convert dollars for some cash before you come, or prior to taking the shuttle-boat when you arrive. As a general rule, 100 CFP is approximately USD$1.

Be Aware: Secure your valuables while snorkeling

When you find yourself in such an idyllic environment, with hardly a soul around, you may put your guard down and think it is unnecessary to use your room's safety deposit box. Especially when you're just going for a swim straight from your overwater bungalow. But we did hear of folk who jumped from their deck for a snorkel and returned to find that someone had stolen money from their wallet, which had been left on the desk.

Save on Accommodation

You've probably already realized that accommodation is the largest cost of a vacation in Bora Bora. Some hotel "rooms" sell for $1800 a night. These villas are so luxurious you wouldn't actually want to miss a moment by closing your eyes to sleep in them!

A vacation in Bora Bora may cost more than some other island destinations people commonly flock to. Its far-out-in-the-Pacific location means that *everything* costs more. But everyone (we know) who has traveled to this exotic isle says their vacation was worth every cent.

Our focus is on how to have a wonderful time visiting legendary Bora Bora, without having to worry about what it's costing! There *are* affordable hotel stays at beautiful resorts. You just need to know what to look for. And yes, some accommodation costs more than you might usually pay, but is well worth booking if you've got the money. So if you want to snag luxury accommodation for a fraction of the price tag the unwitting pay, here are your options:

Go During Low Season

Bora Bora is a small island, with limited accommodation, compared to most destinations. There's a huge difference in hotel prices between the seasons, simply based on supply and demand. July and August are always the *busiest* months in Tahiti.

In July, the Heiva, a month-long festival of art and sporting events, attracts many extra visitors from around the world. During August school is out in Europe and the USA. It's a very popular vacation time for families, and working folk in general, who are also given holidays during this slow period, and escape to paradise.

To avoid high season prices, we recommend going to Bora Bora when there is less demand on accommodation. You will save hundreds (or thousands) of dollars on your resort (and have more island to yourself) by going during low season. You can expect to pay $200 more per night in an overwater bungalow in high season (or save $200 per night by staying in low season).

Select One of the Best Months

There's an important geographical fact to consider while planning. Because Bora Bora is below the equator, low season is during the southern hemisphere's summer months which means it can be hotter and there's a possibility of a higher rainfall. So, here's a valuable secret. *Not all of the summer months are created equal*! We suggest you take advantage of the cheaper prices in the low season months which usually turn on the best weather; *November, May and April.*
Savings: $1600+ (depending on room choice) if you go during low season.

Stay at a Hotel with Easy Access

There are two types of "access" to consider. One is access to shopping and restaurants. The other is access to a sandy beach.

1. Access to Shopping and Eating
It's time for a geography lesson, as Bora Bora is in such a unique setting. There's actually one main island and a scattering of tiny sandy islets (motus) sitting in a calm warm lagoon. The lagoon is formed by a coral-reef necklace of motus that shelter it from the vast Pacific Ocean. Only one narrow entrance allows boats to pass safely in and out through the coral. Volcanic sediment on the shallow, sandy areas of the lagoon floor creates the stunning turquoise hues.

Most luxury resorts are set along perfect white sand beaches, on small islets out in the lagoon; which means that whilst their locations are beautiful and remote, guests are largely limited to the food, shopping, and activities provided at the resort. And their prices! You can save hundreds

16

of dollars during the week by eating at local restaurants, buying drinks from a market, and shopping for souvenirs in the main town of Vaitape. Most resorts charge for the time-tabled, private shuttle service across the lagoon to their dock on the mainland, and some are quite pricey.

Even more inconvenient, if you miss the shuttle you'll have to ring for a (rare and expensive) water taxi! We've experienced being at a restaurant and striking up an interesting conversation with a radio star and his gorgeous model wife, both from South America. While still savoring the main course, he was sharing the insight that life had no meaning for him until he 'found the love'. Suddenly the manager insisted that they must leave the table and get in the free taxi that had been waiting inside, or they would miss the last (9pm) shuttle back to their top resort.

If your intention is to save in every way possible, stay on the mainland of Bora Bora so you can shop at the local markets and dine like the residents. This will also save hundreds on shuttle boat fees getting to and from your resort, on arrival and departure. We explore this area in more detail in the chapters on eating, shopping, and getting around.

2. Access to a Beach

We also want to highlight that the deciding factor when you're comparing, and looking to save on accommodation costs, may actually be *how close the accommodation is to the beach*! Because what makes an island vacation so wonderful is being able to step straight out your door onto an extraordinary beach, at any time of day or night (without having to get there first).

Only some pensions are located next to a beach (Matira), as only part of the coastline on the main island is white-sand, most is rugged. And if (for example) you save big, by staying in the main blocks of rooms at Le Maitai, you must walk down a steep hill and over the Circle Island Road to lounge on its small private beach.

It is possible to visit the beautiful outer motu beaches on Bora Bora through excursions or boat hire. If you stay in a cheaper accommodation option, you will need to factor in the cost of these trips.

Be aware: Not all accommodation located on the coast in Tahiti and Her islands is on an awesome white sand beach. Some budget accommodation may advertise that it's "lagoonside" but is in an area of the lagoon that isn't appealing for swimming because the water is murky and deep. And there's NO BEACH!

For easy access to the beach and dining options, choose between these 3 options:

1. Bora Bora Mainland Resorts

Intercontinental Le Moana
Le Moana has a superb location on Point Matira, opposite Matira beach. We love its romantic beach bungalows and moderately priced overwater bungalows. You can save thousands staying at the *mainland* Intercontinental resort while also enjoying quick and easy free access to the luxurious, sister Intercontinental Resort & Thalasso Spa, on a motu, which has scored many traveler award "bests". Best service. Best spa. Best Mt Otemanu view. Best breakfast (according to us)!

Sofitel Marara Beach
Sofitel Marara Beach is on the main island, just north of Matira Point. There's a variety of food choices, within a 15-minute walk, to keep your food costs down. A glorious infinity swimming pool, bar, and restaurant area has wonderful views across the brilliant lagoon to the Private Island; and all the way to the horizon beyond.

You're also welcome to pay a small boat transfer to get to the Sofitel's more exclusive Private Island Resort and go snorkeling in the Aquarium coral gardens. It's one of the main attractions in Bora Bora. And you can go as often as you wish, for free! If your funds are quite limited, you wouldn't even have to pay for a lagoon snorkeling excursion.
Savings: $200 on a snorkeling excursion

2. Bora Bora's Mainland Budget Hotels

Le Maitai
This more traditional-style hotel offers no added extras, which keeps it very cheap for Bora Bora. Although accommodation is no frills, the views from the upstairs rooms are arguably the best in Bora Bora. It has the bonus of a small private beach with kayaks; which is where the overwater bungalows, the beach bungalows, and a restaurant are located. The standard rooms, reception, and bar are on the other side of the island's only main road; which separates them from the beach.

Matira Hotel
This small, family run, budget hotel is located alongside the public beach at Point Matira; opposite the Intercontinental Le Moana. Its 14 rustic, Polynesian style bungalows are set in an immaculate garden. Each basic hut has a little deck with sun lounges, 2 queen beds, shower, and a fridge. You can find all the food that you'll need, right nearby.

Be aware: The resorts in Bora Bora are the stars! Yes, they're unlike any other hotels in the world. Most "rooms" are exotic over water style villas or thatched-roof beach bungalows. Not even the best of the family pensions offers anything like the luxury, grounds, or beaches that the resorts are renowned for.

3. Motu Resorts with an Easy Shuttle Service:

Intercontinental Thalasso Resort
Intercontinental Thalasso has a frequent, *free* shuttle over to sister resort, Le Moana, at Matira Point. It uses smaller boats and runs them more frequently than most other resorts.

Conrad Bora Bora Nui
Nui Resort has a reasonably priced shuttle service which drops guests off regularly at the main village, Vaitape. The shuttle price is higher in the evenings than during the day, so adds to the cost of going out to dinner.

Pearl Beach Resort
Pearl Beach Resort has a free, 5-minute boat service to its mainland

dock. From there guests can catch a bus into Vaitape.
Savings: $160 on transfers for the week
$250+ on food and drinks

Say No to the Over-Water-Bungalow

No, we haven't forgotten the destination! Yes, the glossy photos and posters featuring thatched-roof bungalows, hovering over turquoise water, have made these huts on stilts synonymous with Bora Bora. But with this one astute choice you can save thousands of dollars. And have a wonderful vacation in far less costly accommodation which also has a charming, pandanas-leaf roof!

There are advantages in staying 'on land'. You'll be closer to the beach, pool, and bar. It's likely you'll have the resort's gorgeous white-sand beach almost to yourself, as everyone in an overwater villa tends to stay there (trying to get their money's worth) while swimming and sunning. From the beach you can take pleasure in looking at the perfect, postcard-picture scenery; which includes overwater villas at each resort.

Free yourself from the notion of having to be *overwater* and there are amazing accommodation options to be found. You can have so much more...while also saving money. For example, a St Regis ocean-front pool villa costs less than an overwater bungalow stay; but offers very private, spacious accommodation, with a generous sized pool, and sweeping ocean views to the horizon.

Stay in a Beach Bungalow

We highly recommend booking a beach bungalow, if you can find the few extra dollars it will cost to step up from a garden bungalow, which is usually an identical villa. To us, this doesn't feel like we're settling for less! You get front row views of your resort's idyllic beach, and at some resorts, even Mt Otemanu.

In Australia, there's a popular sticker saying that "life's a beach". Which may explain why *our* favorite way to stay is in a beach bungalow. This slashes the cost of a vacation in Bora Bora. Choose between the beach bungalows at the following resorts to pay half the price of an overwater bungalow stay:

Le Meridien for Dazzling Views of Mt O

Le Meridien beach bungalows are in a peaceful, private setting at the edge of the resort's inner lagoon; surrounded by palms. You can laze blissfully by the water, right outside your door, with a perfect close-up view of majestic Mt Otemanu directly across the lagoon. These beautifully maintained beach bungalows have a light, airy, modern feeling.

There are a couple of extra spacious bungalows offering 2 bedrooms. If it's possible to share with family or friends, booking a bungalow together would considerably reduce the cost of accommodation, which is usually the biggest chunk of expenditure.

Le Meridien is a good option for those wanting to honeymoon or marry in Bora Bora; on a strict budget. And it's the best priced resort if you are picturing yourself walking down the aisle of a quaint little *overwater chapel*, with a memorable lagoon vista.

Intercontinental Le Moana Oozes Traditional Charm

If you are guarding your dollars but want something special, Le Moana is the entry point for enjoying a luxury stay in Bora Bora. Its elegant beach bungalows combine the charm of traditional Polynesian craftsmanship with gleaming comfort. If you opt to stay here, ask for one that has a view of Mt Otemanu, and is on the quiet south side of beach. You'll get the most value for your money.

These beach bungalows at the mainland resort are the best priced Intercontinental rooms in Bora Bora, and staying at Le Moana has extra perks. There's complimentary boat transport over to the more upmarket, sister resort, Intercontinental Thalasso, on a motu. Thalasso is loaded with French pizzaz and has a sensational beach with a perfect aspect across the lagoon to Mt Otemanu. Buy the Intercontinental breakfast plan and you can choose to boat across to indulge in the sumptuous, international buffet spread at Thalasso.

Le Moana is located on a private section of the island's most popular beach; and has a choice of value-for-money eating places, plus a mini-mart nearby. It's easy to get around from here so there's no need to buy the resort's meal plan.

Pearl Beach for the Prettiest Panorama

Romantic, on the sand bungalows at Pearl Beach offer a polished Robinson Crusoe castaway-on-a-garden-isle experience, for a fraction of the price of sleeping overwater. It's just a few steps across the sand to the shallow, calm lagoon.

At this secluded resort you don't need to pay top dollar to have what may be the prettiest panorama in Bora Bora. From a beach bungalow you enjoy the same spectacular view of the lush, green side of Mt Otemanu (featuring the outline of the Valley of the Kings walk) as the most expensive overwater bungalows. We think these beach bungalows have the loveliest view of any in Bora Bora!

Conrad Nui for Sophisticated Serenity

The Conrad Nui's thatched-roof, beach bungalows are larger, have a more sophisticated decor, and gleam with richly polished timber. They form a row along the edge of the golden sand; at the striking, black lava-rock end of the resort. Each now has its own very private plunge pool, to fit with Nui's rebranding under the classy Conrad flag.

This quiet resort offers the largest selection of watercraft and was the first to provide complimentary paddle board for guests. I seized the opportunity to develop the skill of balancing on a paddle board here, on the calm lagoon. There are snorkeling opportunities around coral along the shoreline, as well as straight from over water bungalows.

Sofitel Marara for Affordable Resort-style

Sofitel Marara has petite beach bungalows, nestled along its vast stretch of white sand. They enjoy a wide front row view across the multi-blue lagoon to Taha'a on the horizon. Along with the garden bungalows, they're part of the original accommodation built to house actors and crew during the making of the movie, "Hurricane". We sat out front imagining the stars lolling around in the very same spot, waiting for their call.

These simple huts exude an earthy, tropical-island ambiance, are proudly cared for, and have everything you need on an island vacation. They're the cheapest priced beach bungalows of any Bora Bora resort. Staying at this part of the main island you also save extra dollars by sourcing food and drinks at nearby cafes, restaurants and mini-mart. As mentioned above, you can also save hundreds on a snorkeling excursion (if you need to) because the famous coral gardens, popularly named the "Aquarium"can be accessed in an outrigger or kayak.

Le Maitai to Save the Most $$

No frills Le Maitai has small, simple, rustic bungalows sitting on sand at the side of its small palm-tree fringed beach. Their Polynesian decor is quite authentic, but a little jaded. On the plus side, they're conveniently located for getting around and sourcing food. They're in close proximity to the Circle Island Road, which can be a little noisy from scooters and cars in the evening and early morning. There's no need to commit money to a meal plan if you stay here. You can stock up your fridge from the nearby mini-market, and it's also an easy (anyone can do) walk to other food choices.

Savings: $4200 compared to an overwater bungalow stay

Choose a Garden Bungalow

To have the luxury of a nice resort to frolic in, while seeing Bora Bora on a low budget, book a garden bungalow. This canl save thousands of dollars compared to staying in an overwater bungalow! The more luxurious the resort, the bigger the savings.

Garden bungalows are the lowest priced rooms available at the resorts. Set amongst lush tropical gardens, with only a few steps to a dreamy, white-sand beach, they offer the most affordable resort style, private-beach vacation in Bora Bora. Take advantage of the fact that a well-priced garden bungalow allows you to enjoy the same gorgeous beach and

23

facilities as the frivolous guests paying top dollar.

Garden bungalows are the lowest priced resort rooms in Bora Bora.

Savings: $6000 (compared to an overwater bungalow stay).

Garden Rooms to Choose From:

Conrad Nui

Conrad Nui has 16 **Lagoon View Suites** in 'hotel block' style accommodation with a thatched roof. They have lovely vistas over the dark-blue, deep water at this part of the lagoon. Each suite has the same spacious layout and quality furnishings as most of the pricier, individual Nui bungalows. We've compared them!

Conrad Nui's **Horizon View Villas** are the next level up in pricing. Speaking of *up*, they're perched on the hillside, overlooking the beautiful flowering gardens and the lagoon. If you want lots of privacy you'll have it here. A stay in one of these exotic tree houses is quite out of the ordinary. They are at varying heights so if you don't wish to climb up lots of stairs, ask for one lower down with less steps to negotiate.

Conrad Nui offers **Garden Villas** similar to the 2 types described above. Set in lush gardens, they cost a little more because they're closer to the beach and facilities.

Pearl Beach Resort

Pearl Beach is *the* garden resort. It's no surprise that their **Garden Pool Villas** each have a shady veranda with a dining area overlooking a large leafy garden, featuring a private plunge pool; all within the quiet seclusion of a surrounding bamboo wall. There's even an outdoor bathroom.

Sofitel Marara Beach Resort

Marara Beach has 29_**Garden Bungalows**. Each "hotel room" is a separate hut, set privately amongst flowering gardens. Charming walkways, adorned by tropical foliage, lead to the enticing beach. Staying here means you can also save hundreds of dollars on a snorkeling excursion. A small charge for boat transfer to the Private Island Resort allows you to create your own free expedition, rowing to the popular Coral Gardens for snorkeling.

Le Maitai

Le Maitai has **Garden View rooms** and **Ocean View rooms** in basic hotel style blocks with thatched roofs. They're perched high on a hill, above the reception area so the walkway to the rooms is up a steep incline, overlooking exotic gardens. The views make the walk worthwhile.

As Le Maitai is the very cheapest hotel style stay in Bora Bora I am going to add in some more details.

Le Matai's **Ocean View rooms** are on the top floor, offering the most extraordinary panorama of the lagoon's kaleidoscope of blues (that you'll see outside of a helicopter). The world's finest camera cannot capture the magnitude of this dream-like vista. Even when I'm seeing it I can't believe it! This accommodation has an *empty* fridge which enables you to save more by stocking up on food from the mini-mart that's a short walk up the road. You can also save money on breakfasts and lunches by putting together your own. Step out to the balcony for the best eating location in Bora Bora. You just have to provide your own service.

The **Garden View rooms** on the lower levels of the Maitai are an even cheaper option here, as you pay a little more for the awesome water views upstairs. These are the cheapest hotel rooms in Bora Bora offering a private beach with watercraft! However, we think it's worth parting with the few extra dollars for an Ocean View room because, unlike most advertised properties, the sensational "bird's eye" water view of the world's most beautiful lagoon is so wide and grand.

If You Can't Say No to an Overwater Bungalow...

OK. We understand. It's Bora Bora and this is an unbelievably blue, warm lagoon! You've been eyeing off those little thatched huts perched over water for years, and this trip may be a once in a lifetime vacation experience! So if you're juggling money, we've done the homework for you, and here are your choices:

Select One of Bora Bora's Cheapest!

Le Maitai

If staying *over* water is a *must*, but you *must* also keep your accommodation costs down, **Le Maitai** hotel offers modest overwater bungalows for a tiny fraction of the cost of staying in luxury at Bora Bora resorts. They have an authentic Polynesian feel that smacks more of 'traditional Tahiti' than *luxury* resort. Some are near the shore, quite close to the little beach where guests paddle into the water with kayaks.

I've often supposed that if you haven't experienced the luxurious ones you wouldn't know the difference. We've seen very happy holidaymakers on their decks, excitedly pointing out passing marine life to us, as we rowed by. If you don't arrive with expectations of basking in luxury, these budget priced overwater huts may be the answer to your prayers. Don't bother about a meal plan. From here it's a short walk to a choice of food which will be cheaper (and probably tastier).

Sofitel Marara Beach

The Sofitel offers the first overwater bungalows that were built in Bora Bora. But don't think you can dive from the deck of these! They're priced low because they back onto the shore, with only their front legs in the lagoon, and they're amongst the smallest on the island. These were added when the director's daughter turned the site into a hotel after completion of the filming of Hurricane.

Later, another row was constructed further out, also in shallow water, and booking one of these means big savings also. Spectacular views across the water, in the area of the lagoon which has the wildest blue hues, give this resort a big tick. Plus it's easy to get around the island from here.

Yacht Club

The simple bungalows that Bora Bora Yacht Club has built over water are a fairly recent, affordable addition. They are in a deeper part of the lagoon so the blue of the water is naturally darker, instead of the vibrant turquoise that usually leaps out of Bora Bora photos. If you've been dreaming of jumping off your deck into soft sand and iridescent blue water, these are not the bungalows for you.

In their favor, this west side of the island has wonderful views of the sun setting over the Pacific Ocean. Plus the fresh, flavorsome food at the Yacht Club is well priced, so there's a great restaurant right nearby. We've seen fish being loaded straight off the boats and into the kitchen, making this the place to get the freshest fish dish. Ask for your pina colada to be made with freshly squeezed coconut milk.

Staying here you'll meet interesting characters traveling through from far off corners of the planet and be entertained by the yarns they spin. In the evenings, the bar has a convivial air as locals come here to gossip and socialize alongside of visitors.

Intercontinental Le Moana

Le Moana delivers a delightful touch of glamor, without the price tag of staying overwater at 4 or 5 star resorts. Its elegant, airy, overwater bungalows are sitting above shallow, clear, turquoise water, with a soft sandy floor. This smaller, more modest, but immaculately maintained Intercontinental on the main island of Bora Bora displays beautiful craftsmanship by Polynesian artisans.

We mentioned above that Matira point is a convenient area because there's a variety of shops and restaurants nearby, as well as Matira Beach across the road. Staying here means you can eat free-range, without being dependent on costly resort meal plans (we'll talk more about this in the eating section) or limited transport schedules. You're likely to save money on getting around the island too.

Buy the Le Moana breakfast buffet and you can choose to indulge in a huge international feast laid out at the more up-market InterContinental on an outer motu of Bora Bora. The free, frequent shuttle boat over to the sister resort, Thalasso, adds extra value. It's an open invitation to shop (but don't!), dine, and visit the awesome Deep Ocean Spa. Just book one treatment (imagine having a massage while watching the lagoon life swim by underneath) and get complimentary use of the splendid outdoor water treatments for a whole morning or afternoon. Plus anytime you like, you can enjoy the motu beach, with its up-close-and-personal Mt Otemanu backdrop.

Savings: $4200

Sleep Only 2 Nights Overwater

Are you wanting to keep costs down, but your dream is to have a rendezvous in one of those little huts over the lagoon? Sleep just 2 nights overwater (which gives a whole day to play) and have the remainder of your stay on land. It's an effective strategy if you're leaning towards a resort whose price for overwater accommodation would otherwise put it out of reach. This simple move makes a luxurious overwater bungalow experience possible for astute travelers with a small budget.

Savings: $4250

Say No to a Mt Otemanu View

You've probably noticed that travel writers (including us) make a big fuss about majestic Mt Otemanu being the "signature peak". Such alluring mystery has been created around this sturdy outcrop of rock which has withstood the elements of time! It's probably contributed to inflating the price of a room with a view of the black basalt rock protruding above Bora Bora's lush, green vegetation.

You can keep thousands in your pocket by opting for an overwater bungalow *without* a Mt Otemanu view. Your tropical island outlook will either be across the glistening lagoon or towards the gorgeous palm-tree fringed beach of your resort. Who couldn't be happy with that? Most resorts offer superb views of Bora Bora Island and its rocky towers from around their grounds, and you're likely to be outside during most daylight hours. To make huge savings on overwater accommodation, put a view of Mt Otemanu low on your priorities.

The Otemanu view overwater bungalows also tend to be the ones furthest out from the resort facilities. This makes it a long walk when you have to grab something from your room. And the ones with the best views are usually further out where the water is deeper and there's more likelihood of a current flowing by. There are plenty of advantages to staying closer to the beach.
Savings: $2800

Sleep Overwater on Another Island

If you have your heart set on an overwater bungalow, but are looking for one well under $1000 per night, compare those that are available on Tahiti and Moorea. An overwater bungalow on Bora Bora averages between $600 and $1200/night. You can find a beautiful one for half that price on Moorea and Tahiti. It's the supply and demand principle. But we don't recommend those on the main island of Tahiti as a substitute for staying over the tranquil Bora Bora lagoon! Moorea offers lovely bungalows, in scenic locations, that come very close.
Savings: $900 by staying over water on another island for 2 nights.

The main island of Tahiti has much to explore. Black sand beaches! A large lush inner island with waterfalls! But its lagoon is different to those in the other Society islands like Bora Bora. Don't think that staying in an overwater bungalow on the main island of Tahiti will be like a stay in one on Bora Bora.

Rent a Private Overwater Villa

Bora Bora's main island has a few privately-owned overwater bungalows available for rent. There are two at the north end of the island, facing across deep blue water towards the airport motu. They're known as Marlon Brando's, as he was the famous previous owner. The friendly local

29

manager Nir (who also owns pension villas) picks guests up on arrival and settles them in.

If you're independent minded people, renting one of these large 2 bedroom villas affords lots of privacy, and you can swim in the crystal-clear water, straight from the bungalow. But from this part of the island, it's a long way round to shop, eat, and explore the only public beach, Matira, which is at the southern tip of the island. So to get around easily, at your leisure, you would need to hire a car, for some of your time. Although that adds to the cost of the trip, remember that you're avoiding resort prices.

The only common issue that guests raise about these overwater bungalows is that the lounge chairs are too firm! So if you want to save money by having a second bedroom, and value the freedom to eat and explore independently, one of these could suit you.
Savings: $3150

Don't Book All-inclusive Unless...

The only time to book an "all inclusive" deal is if you see a Bora Bora resort offering a special promotion which includes a meal plan. We once bought a package immediately when the Scoupon deal offer came to our in-box. The Bora Bora Nui (now the Conrad) was offering 7 nights of accommodation, boat transfers, *and* a full meal plan, for less than what accommodation would normally cost.

Upon arrival at the Nui, we were informed that rooms were overbooked, and so we were serendipitously upgraded. During the week we tried every dish on the menu, without needing to give a thought to cost. At lunchtime, the restaurant manager allowed us (small eaters) to come back later for our desert, so each afternoon we savored our ice-cream sundaes under a palm tree on the beach.

Although we would not have had to leave the resort for food, we caught the shuttle over to the main island to try out the Kaina Hut, and it didn't feel like we were being extravagant by paying out extra.

Great deals like this only come up occasionally. In the past couple of years, I have seen one for the Pearl Beach Bora Bora and another for a stay at the Kia Ora Resort & Spa in Rangiroa. Sometimes, to take advantage of exceptional accommodation deals, you need to be flexible about the time you travel. Check flight availability and prices *before* you book a hotel to ensure that you can purchase fine priced fares to correspond with your hotel booking.

Savings: $4000 plus by booking a special deal

Stay Between Sister Resorts

Staying between resorts of the same chain, throughout Tahiti, can take hundreds of dollars off your total vacation cost. To have a special package like this, you will need to book with a Tahiti travel agent.

Stay at the Pearl Beach hotel set on a black sand beach, north of Papeete, when you fly in to or out of Tahiti, and then at the Pearl Beach Resort in Bora Bora. The Taha'a Resort is also affiliated so you'll get at least 20% off an interlude over there.

Stay at the Hilton in Moorea and the Conrad Nui at Bora Bora.
Choose one of the Intercontinental Resorts in Bora Bora - Thalasso or Le Moana - and you can also make big savings on a night at the Intercontinental in Tahiti as you arrive and leave. It's fairly close to the airport.

If you plan to visit Moorea you will also benefit by booking the Intercontinental there. Starwood Hotels offer the St Regis and Le Meridien in Bora Bora, plus a Le Meridian on the main island of Tahiti, south of Papeete.

Savings: $800 by combining stays between sister resorts

Split Your Stay Between Islands

You've probably heard Bora Bora referred to as the "Pearl of the Pacific". Its seductive allure makes the limited hotel accommodation more expensive. So if you are coming to French Polynesia for more than 4 nights, consider visiting another island in combination with Bora Bora.

There are other islands close to Bora Bora that are beautiful in their own right *and* offer accommodation for less than the price of staying on Bora Bora. This is an especially good strategy if you are coming to Tahiti for a week or more. Our top pick of islands include Moorea, Le Taha'a, and Huahine. And if you have the time and dollars, and are seeking adventure, we highly recommend flying out to the Tuamotu Atolls. *Refer to the Resources section* to see what's best about each suggestion.

Take into account that traveling between islands usually involves a short plane flight and, as there is only one inter-island carrier, there is no competition to make flight prices competitive. See the section on 'flights' to find out *how to fly between a few islands while only paying a little more than a return flight to Bora Bora costs.*
Savings: $2400 by combining nights on another island

Stay in a Pension or Guest House

If your budget is lower than the previous options, check out the Bora Bora pensions offering a variety of bed & breakfast style accommodation. This is a stay in a local home, room, or guest house, with breakfast or a basic kitchen provided. A few simply provide a bed and a fridge. Others provide guests with a pickup from the airport boat-shuttle dock at Vaitape, and welcome guests into their home, lending bicycles and even escorting them around the island. Some also have meals on offer.

Hosts may be French ex-patriots or Polynesian. If you don't speak French, before you choose one, have sufficient conversation with a prospective host to check that you will be able to communicate adequately. You'll want to ask questions about the island and you won't have a hotel concierge to help you out during your vacation.

If you choose a pension stay you *may* have beach access near the property. But most home-stays on Bora Bora's main island are located in areas of the island that *don't* have a beach. So guests go to Matira, which is not too far from anywhere on this small island.

You can get warm Polynesian hospitality staying at a pension but you won't have as many facilities as at a resort. So before you leap into saving money by choosing a pension or guest house, you must compare that experience with a resort stay. Be congruent about what will give *you* the type of vacation that you've been hoping for. You may even decide to save a little longer to have what you want.

Let's Compare What You Get for Your $$

At this time most of the pensions have not been rated by the official Tahiti organization which awards tiares for stars, so they have to be evaluated by experience.

Firstly, let's have a look at an example from the **top of the range**, whose status is not only reflected in the price, but by the fact it has officially been granted 3 tiares. **Rhotu Fare** is probably the best that's available if you are looking for a private stay. It's home to Nir and his family, and also has several unusual, thatched-roof guest cottages, each with their own kitchenette and bathroom. The main bedroom features a huge carved-log four poster bed and some of the bungalows offer an extra bedroom with twin beds.

These arty, thatched roof, wood and bamboo huts have an out of the ordinary, sensual decor and they're a little dim inside. They're set amongst exotic tropical trees on the mountain side, south of Vaitape. From their decks there are views over the island and the village of Vaitape. They **sell from 250 Euros (U.S.$280)** for a couple, per night.

Rhotu Fare advertises that it's located just 250 meters (600 feet) from the Circle Island Road and lagoon. That sounds as if it's just a short walk down to the lagoon for a swim. But unfortunately there is no beach at this part of the island! You will have to go to Matira. Which means arranging a lift with Nir, borrowing one of the complimentary bicycles, or a l-o-n-g walk. (By the time you get back you'll be wanting another swim!)

We think this island is all about the palm-tree studded white-sand beaches fringing the most vibrantly blue lagoon. What attracts us back is being able to step out of our room and *be* at the lagoon. It makes our Bora Bora vacation! So a private hide-away in the jungle would not be amongst our first choices. But it might be yours.

To find a pension or guest house near the beach, you'll have to choose from those located at Matira, the only public beach on the main island of Bora Bora.

At the low end of the scale there is some very basic accommodation. Travelers with dollar constraints who just want to see the world's most beautiful island, on an extreme budget (and don't demand any luxury), can have a room in a house with a shared bathroom for about US$100; depending on the season.

Pension Robert Et Tina is an example of what's available at the backpacker end of the accommodation scale. Set at the tip of point Matira, it's owned by a Polynesian family who have 3 separate houses with a total of 15 rooms. Don't book expecting any kind of comforts, (let alone luxury) despite the price tag which doesn't actually sound all that cheap. On the bright side, you can step out to dazzling Matira Beach, and there are shops and a choice of eating places right nearby.

But there are absolutely no indulgences here. It's a place to lay down your head at night. There's a small communal kitchen with simple equipment. The shared bathroom spurts *COLD* water from the taps. Your room is basic, and you have no area to sit (after breakfast is over) except your room or balcony. There's no watercraft to use (or even hire at the pension), no Wi-Fi, no air con, and not much English.

If you're going for a special occasion; like your honeymoon, wedding, anniversary, or crossing Bora Bora off your bucket list; you're looking for something better. Most pensions just cater for the adventure travel market, by providing a base for experiencing the island and its legendary lagoon.

Check Listings on AirBnB

Islanders are opening up their homes on Airbnb, with room prices as low as $60 a night! There are also whole houses available for rent. Accommodation options vary from small rooms in Vaitape village to a whole house and private pool, on a motu, facing the ocean. Do look closely at the descriptions, pictures and reviews.

Beware: If you take this independent option you are without the assistance of a travel agent to fix problems, or a concierge service to help with excursions, or a shuttle boat schedule to get you to the mainland when you want to go

If its accommodation is on a motu, check that there's a complimentary boat service to the main island, and whether any meals are included. Once you're on a tiny motu in Bora Bora's lagoon, it's as if you're on a deserted island! That may sound like the break you are looking for but it just might break you. If you want a drink or snack after your dip in the lagoon, there won't be anywhere nearby to get one!

Be aware: A booking at one of these is not as secure as a hotel booking. They set the rules and have the right to cancel if they wish. If you suddenly found you were without accommodation it would cost a fortune to find something else at the last minute. Some ask for hundreds of dollars for a deposit. (Whereas hotels keep your credit card details.) Check what the security deposit is before deciding on one of these

Say No to Extras and Frills

For most of those whom fortune rewards with a vacation in Bora Bora, it's a once in a lifetime experience. But that shouldn't mean that you have to spend the rest of your life paying for it! Adopting a savvy attitude will prepare you to resist unnecessary temptations that would otherwise break your budget. Instead you'll save hundreds of dollars. Think of it as self-respect rather than a feat of self-discipline or self-denial.

While planning your trip you will hear of things (you didn't even know exist) to spend money on. If you choose a travel agent, make sure it's one who has personally vacationed in Bora Bora (a number of times). One who understands that each resort is located on such a spectacular beach and offers enough recreational activities, that there's no need to spend much extra at all. The right travel agent will guide you on "must dos" but not talk you into extravagances with expectations or assumptions around how *your* hard-earned money should be spent.

Be warned that in paradise resorts specialize in creating out-of-this-world experiences. While you're on vacation, surrounded by awesome beauty and a little drunk from the island air (or French wine), it's easy to lose touch with reality. After all, you've already laid out considerable money so why not a little more? It's the vacation of a lifetime! We have been programmed to think that we deserve what is on offer, and not having it is depriving ourselves. You may also feel pressured to treat or impress your partner. Remind yourself (kindly) that managing your money is much more satisfying and impressive!

I know from experience! It's easy to sip the 2 for one happy hour cocktails and start calculating how much you will save if you buy 2 more! Or you see breakfast being delivered to the deck of a neighboring overwater bungalow, by flower decorated canoe. It's a colorful sight to behold. But it's not necessary for it to be *yours* to enjoy that magic moment of lagoon ambiance. Take a photograph. Put it on Facebook. Enjoy it all the more because you are entertained by a vision that someone else is paying for. Then remember how much fun it is lingering over the buffet in the panoramic breakfast room where there are actually more choices (for less)! It's special just sitting on any deck in Bora Bora, nibbling from the selection of mini-mart food that you've squirreled away in the fridge.

Get a Free Room and More

Grasping this exciting topic makes it possible to prepare for huge savings by strategically setting yourself up for entitlements, privileges, and freebies, ahead of your holiday. It's one more reason to get in early with organizing your travel to Bora Bora!

Residents of North America are probably already aware that they can sign up for credit cards to take advantage of significant bonus offers that come with them. Knowing the entitlements each provides may actually be a decisive factor in choosing your resorts for a Tahiti vacation. Three main hotel groups in French Polynesia offer a point system to reward customer loyalty:

1. The Intercontinental Hotel Group

- Intercontinental Thalasso Bora Bora
- Intercontinental Le Moana Bora Bora
- Intercontinental Resort Tahiti
- Intercontinental Resort & Spa Moorea

IHG Reward Club Select has the lowest annual fee ($49) for a hotel credit card which offers an annual free night certificate. It's also the only hotel credit card which offers a free night without a cap on the category of hotel you can redeem it at.

Between the IHG Reward Club Select credit card, and the program's promotions, it's easy to accumulate points if you're loyal to the Intercontinental hotel chain. This particular card is also worthwhile because it has *no international transaction fees*. When you're spending in Tahiti, you'll keep a worthwhile amount of money in your pocket simply from not accumulating annoying, additional bank charges.

As an elite member you can ask for an upgrade, and hope. But consider that *members who have Ambassador status are guaranteed a room upgrade*. Even one tier qualifies at the two Intercontinental hotels in Bora Bora. To attain *Ambassador* status you can either part with 32,000 points or pay $200 for the status. You'll probably find it cheaper to spend the $200 rather than paying to upgrade for even one night. It's worth being Ambassador just for the other benefits and privileges, like free Wi-Fi and priority check-in, even though its status is only recognized when you stay at Intercontinental hotels.

When you take out the credit card you get 80,000 points completely complimentary. So if you decide to stay at Intercontinental hotels while in Tahiti, ensure that *both* you and your partner sign up for the card to instantly acquire 160,000 points. Then, before you pack your bags for Tahiti, make sure that one of you upgrades to *Ambassador* so that you qualify for a room upgrade.

2. Hilton Hotels & Resorts
- Conrad Nui
- Hilton Moorea

The Hilton Honors Reserve Card is currently the Hilton card offering most benefits for those planning to stay at a Hilton resort on a future Tahiti vacation. When you are granted a card you automatically receive Gold Status, and by spending $2,500 on purchases within the first 4 months you're given 2 weekend night certificates for a standard room. This is worth hundreds, just at the Bora Bora Nui so the $95 cost for the card becomes quite insignificant. Keep in mind that you're also rewarded with another bonus weekend night at each yearly anniversary of being a card holder.
The Reserve card also meets our criteria as it's the only Hilton credit card that *waives conversion rate bank fees* on foreign transactions. The other Hilton credit cards will charge you a conversion rate between 2.7% and 3% per transaction when you use them outside of the United States, so any rewards you earn from them will be severely reduced by this unnecessary fee.

If you acquire Hilton Gold Elite Status, you also *save $32 per person on breakfast* at the Bora Bora and Moorea resorts. Feasting over breakfast at the Moorea Hilton is an experience in itself! An enormous international buffet is laid out in an airy, thatched roof building, especially designed to capture wrap-around views of some of the world's most glorious scenery.

The combination of perks make the Hilton accommodation options extra appealing for those who want a real Tahiti style vacation, with luxury thrown in; without an enormous price tag. You could enjoy your overwater experience at the gorgeous Hilton Moorea which costs much less than in Bora Bora, even though we find it just as beautiful. The beachfront villas at Moorea also have a superb ambiance and outlook.

At the Bora Bora Nui, a lagoon view suite will be a standard room. These suites offer the same spacious layout as the villas, and have the same elegant furnishings and huge, luxurious bathroom. They're lighter and brighter because they have white walls instead of the natural materials that were used for the separate villas. You can have your free night in one of these lovely suites and make big savings.

3. Starwood Hotels
- St Regis Bora Bora
- Le Meridien Bora Bora
- Le Meridien Tahiti

The Starwood Preferred Guest credit card from American Express also has above average ratings. However it's not because of the amount of points earned for each dollar spent but due to the extra perks that come with it. To reach SPG Gold you need to accumulate either 10 stays or 25 nights in a calendar year. Or if you spend at least $30,000 per year on your card, you'll receive automatic Gold status plus credit for 2 stays and 5 nights. It's structured so that a member typically needs to spend $6,972 to receive a free one-night stay. This is about $4,810 higher than the average for all hotel rewards.

But you'll find that *Bora Bora Le Meridien always has special offers* that are exclusively for Starwood Preferred Guests, provided you book directly with them. As I am writing this SPGs enjoy:
- Staying from 25,350 XPF + taxes per night
- Double Starpoints
- Every 4th night complimentary
- 20% off dining discount

Complimentary in-room premium internet access ($15 savings per night) Some special offers are for a limited time frame. Currently Le Meridien is offering members of the Starwood Preferred Guest program 50% off rack rates on premium room categories for travel until the end of the year.

Get More for Less with an Upgrade

Here are strategies to help get an upgrade:

You can use status *and* loyalty points when asking for an upgrade. If you're going in low season it's more likely that you'll have the good fortune of the resort confirming your upgrade soon after they receive your request.

If they do not upgrade you based on status, contact the resort again. If, in the reply, the hotel doesn't provide prices for upgrading, politely email back asking how much it will cost to upgrade from the room which you currently have booked to what you prefer e.g. an overwater bungalow. Provide specific details about your current booking so they can respond with an accurate price.

You can also try using points when asking for an upgrade. If you don't have quite enough it's likely that purchasing the extra, necessary points will cost less than paying for the room outright. We have found that most resorts don't apply points directly towards an overwater bungalow. They provide a villa on the property which you can redeem points for, and then ask you to pay cash if you want an upgrade to an overwater bungalow.

One Bora Bora hotel stands out as offering the best value when redeeming points. Are you aware that *all rooms are overwater bungalows* at the Intercontinental Thalasso? An overwater bungalow is a standard room at this luxurious resort! So you can have one for only 50,000 points. Even at the other French Polynesian IHG resorts (and all other Bora Bora resorts) you would have to upgrade after your initial points payment, to get an overwater bungalow.

While selecting your hotel accommodation, check for current promotions on Flyertalk threads. For example, on the IHG thread you could find something as exciting as a code for 'free Ambassador' which scores an upgrade to a Diamond room in Bora Bora.

Take a Cruise

Cruising is *the most 'all inclusive' option* for a vacation in Tahiti. Even tailored drink plans are available for a bargain price. Excursions can be pre-booked through the cruise portal or, if you want to save at least 20%, you can do it yourself. You know upfront *exactly* how much you will be spending.

I've saved thousands of dollars seeing Tahiti by cruise ship. Several times. Yet when I booked my first trip to French Polynesia I didn't even consider myself someone who would cruise. I was quite young and thought that a vacation in Bora Bora was beyond my means, until I discovered that my Mileage Plus frequent flyer points could get me there (from Australia) with Air New Zealand. There's lots more info about this in the flight section.

While searching for affordable accommodation I wrestled over prices. Quite unexpectedly I stumbled upon a Princess Line cruise that fitted my time frame. This made it possible to see Bora Bora *and five other pristine islands*, at a bargain price. With travel between islands, accommodation, meals and entertainment all provided!

One serendipitous choice enabled me to avoid expensive accommodation, meals and inter-island airfares. My girlfriend and I went with our boyfriends, so the free nightly entertainment saved us many more dollars, compared to what we might otherwise have spent.

That cruise taught me that *Tahiti* cruises aren't just for old folk and those who are logistically challenged! French Polynesia consists of a group of far flung isles and atolls. So the most natural way to get around is by boat. I discovered that traversing the mighty Pacific, getting up each morning to spot a speck of island on the horizon, appealed to my adventurous spirit. When the ship slowly navigated through the narrow pass into the magical Bora Bora lagoon I felt like an ancient explorer in a foreign land. The islanders rushed out to watch our ship come in, as they don't get many sailing by each year. Now I know that there are *cruises* and there are *Tahiti* cruises!

Smaller **Princess Line** ships sail to Bora Bora several times a year on 11 night voyages.This is simply the most cost effective way to see a few Tahitian islands, with 2 whole days in Bora Bora. There are many other bonuses. Like the time saved not having to pack up and move, be at the airport hours before flights, or wait for transfers to the next hotel.

Paul Gauguin cruises offer more luxurious options for those with bigger

41

budgets. This purpose-built vessel inhabits French Polynesian waters all year round. It offers special itineraries enabling travelers to sail (in great comfort) far out to some of Tahiti's most exotic islands and atolls, where the pearl farms are. You'll *save big money compared to hiring a yacht* and arranging a similar itinerary. All Gauguin cruise packages include airfares, a night in a Papeete hotel on arrival, transfers, meals, open bar, nightly entertainment, and excursions.

Cruising Tahiti is like taking a floating hotel to fantasy islands. Cruise lines use smaller boats here to sail in and approach fragile islands, nestled in the sanctuary of shallow lagoons. It's the most relaxing way to visit a few islands, and make friends along the way. There's no repacking and rushing to airports. You simply go to sleep at night and wake up with a new island to explore.

Savvy Savings on Flights

You're flying halfway across the Pacific to an almost uninhabited area of the planet. Not many people live here and not many tourists get out here, so it's an area with little traffic. If you can find an airfare for around the $1000 mark, you have done well.

The cheapest airfares to Tahiti, that are offered all year, are for short stays. These international flights do come with a condition. They limit the number of nights you are allowed to stay in French Polynesia.

Contrary to the competition that we are accustomed to, Tahiti (and all of French Polynesia) has only one domestic airline, *Air Tahiti*. To get cheaper fares with Air Tahiti, the only inter-island carrier, you must book well ahead. Locals get special rates. So further on we'll tell you how to "become a local".

You may be able to use your departure date as leverage for making more savings on the cost of flights. Airline pricing is based on the season of the departure date for all flights during the trip. If you have to go in high season, try and figure out how to leave a couple of days before it begins. This is one more reason to get in early with booking.

We want to emphasize that the single best strategy for getting cheap flights to Bora Bora is to *book your vacation very early.* If you're staying four or five star, talk with a *reputable Tahiti specialist* who has access to wholesale rates. Book a year ahead if possible.

Best Ways to Save on Your Flights:

1. Use points
2. Fly in the low season
3. Buy the 5 night "Short Stay" airfare
4. Use the low season 6-9 night airfare (Ia Orana fare)
5. Get a free business class companion ticket

6. Buy an Island Hopper pass
7. Take the free ferry from the airport
8. Make Tahiti a stopover

Cheap International Flights

Use Miles for Flights to Bora Bora

As flights to Tahiti usually cost more to purchase than equivalent frequent flyer zones, this is a great destination to milk the most value from your frequent flier miles. Airlines structure reward flights according to zones. With Tahiti falling into the Pacific zone, you usually surrender the same points to fly *anywhere* in this vast ocean of islands. (Sometimes Hawaii is a separate zone).

Consider these two examples: if an American is actually *paying* for tickets to Tahiti they will cost much more than to Hawaii; and if an Australian is purchasing tickets to Tahiti they will cost much more than to Fiji.
Only a few airlines fly into Tahiti, so first you must realize that there is a limited number of seats available to buy. Plus each airline only marks a *limited number of award seats on each flight.* So you will want to book your award travel as far ahead as possible.

Here's the good news. Although only a handful of airlines fly into Papeete (on the main island of Tahiti): Air Tahiti, Air France, Air New Zealand, LATAM, and Hawaiian; they have alliances with a number of partner airlines. You may be able you to use your points with one of those.
Savings: $2000+

How to Fly Free!

I used "miles" to make my very first trip to Tahiti possible. By using my accumulated Mileage Plus points I had a free flight to Tahiti, with only a small payment for taxes (around $150). I never would have been able to afford that first trip without my accumulated frequent flier miles! As United is part of the Star Alliance group, I was able to book a flight to Tahiti with Air New Zealand (which is one of my favorite, as it has the friendliest staff and best quality food).

The flight to Tahiti was simply the best way to use my star alliance points, as the actual number of points to any South Pacific destination is the same. For example, it is 45,000 points to anywhere in the Pacific from Australia. A flight to Tahiti from Australia would cost between $1200 and $2000 dollars. But a flight to Fiji can be bought for only $400. I get at least three times the value from my points by flying to Tahiti.

Check out the frequent flyer programs you are a member of, and how many points it will take to fly to Tahiti. Overseas trips are the most effective way to use points in terms of cost to point ratio. It will take the same number of points, whatever state you live in and fly from.

Redeeming points as a way of getting to Tahiti from North America is easy with American Airlines or Delta frequent flyer programs.

- **American Airlines** partners with Air Tahiti Nui and Hawaiian Airlines.
- **Delta** partners with Air France and Air Tahiti Nui, both of which offer a non-stop service from the U.S. mainland to Tahiti. So Delta is generally the preferable program for Tahiti redemptions.
- **Tahiti Nui** and **Air France** are the *only* airlines providing a non-stop service to Tahiti from the west coast of the United States, so these are the best airlines to fly with.

Main Options for Flying to Tahiti Using Points:

Air France
For those **traveling from Europe, or North America**, flying with Air France using points is an option.
- Air France has about 4 services per week to Tahiti.
- Seven, or even more, award, economy seats can be available (book ahead).
- Business class award space is limited.
- Air France is a SkyTeam member airline, so you can redeem miles from any of the 20 SkyTeam partners including Delta and KLM. Air France also partners with Alaska Mileage Plan and JAL Mileage Bank.

- A typical economy rewards ticket from North America to Papeete starts from 30,000 reward miles.
- A flex-economy ticket starts from 180,000 points.

Air Tahiti Nui

Flying with Air Tahiti Nui using points is an option for those traveling from **North America**.

- As Tahiti's own international airline, they have the most flights to Tahiti, and fly daily between LA and Papeete.
- Usually 4 economy award seats are available per flight, and 2 business class award seats.
- Air Tahiti Nui partners with American Airlines and Delta SkyMiles.
- Codeshare partners include: American Airlines, Qantas, Air New Zealand, Air France, Japan Airlines, Korean Airlines, Aircalin and TGVAir. But not all codeshare partners allow you to use your points with Air Tahiti Nui. For example: Qantas is a partner, but does not show Tahiti as a destination on their awards calculator.
- An economy class one way ticket can be booked for 40,000 points; business class for 80,000; first class for 120,000.

Hawaiian Airlines

Hawaiian is an option for those coming from **Australia and North America**.

- Hawaiian flies once a week between Honolulu and Tahiti.
- Flying with Hawaiian Airlines will require you to travel through Honolulu to Tahiti.
- Hawaiian Airlines partner with: JetBlue, Virgin America and Virgin Australia, All Nippon Airways Mileage Club, American Airlines AAdvantage, Delta SkyMiles, Korean Airlines Skypass, United Airlines Mileage Plus.
- An easy way to find award space on Hawaiian is by searching with the American Airlines AA.com award calendar.
- If you are a Pualani Platinum, Pualani Gold, Premier Club Member, and Hawaiian Airlines MasterCard holder; you have access to additional discounted flight *awards* for travel on Hawaiian Airlines.
- The lowest mileage coach flight award for a one-way trip between Tahiti and North America is 47,50 points.

When the lowest coach flight award is not available, a coach saver award may be purchased online for 72,500 points.

- If neither of the saver awards are available, then a coach flex award ticket can be purchased for double the fare at 95,000 points.
- Upgrades are also available for first class.

Air New Zealand

This is the best option for **Australians, New Zealanders and those coming from the South Pacific** area. Air New Zealand rewards are a fantastic way to travel to Tahiti from Australia and New Zealand as the number of points required is very reasonable for the price of a Tahiti airfare. What's really special about Air New Zealand's rewards program is that if there's a seat for sale on any Air New Zealand ticketed and operated flight, and you have enough Airpoints in your account, you can redeem it!

All Air New Zealand flights pass through New Zealand, the base. Air New Zealand is also an option for those flying from the USA. You would just have to fly to New Zealand before heading to Tahiti.

- 595 Air New Zealand Airpoints required for flying from Australia to Tahiti
- 450 Airpoints between New Zealand and Tahiti
- 745 Airports between North America and Tahiti
- 1,095 Airpoints between Europe and Tahiti

Air New Zealand is a Star Alliance member airline, so if you have award points with United Mileage Plus or a partner airline you can also travel on Air New Zealand using your points. All amounts are for one direction of travel. If you are flying round-trip, just double the mileage amount.

United Mileage Plus Points
There are 2 reward fare types with United Airline's program:

1. **Saver Awards** can be used for travel almost anywhere United, and their MileagePlus airline partners fly. Saver Awards are capacity-controlled and may not be available on certain flights where demand is high. For economy Saver Awards between North America and Tahiti 35,000 reward points are required. Between Australia/NZ and Tahiti 22,500 are required.

2. **Standard Awards** offer greater availability on flights operated by United and are subject to limited capacity controls. While seats for award travel may not be available on certain flights, there are more seats available for Standard Awards than for Saver Awards. Between North America and Tahiti 75,000 Standard reward points are required. Between Australia/NZ and Tahiti 40,000 points are required.

Using Star Alliance Award Points
Here are the miles you need for a Star Alliance/Partner Award.
- 35,000 award points between North America and Tahiti for economy class.
- 22,500 award points Between Australia/NZ and Tahiti for economy class.

Note: The above numbers were correct at time of writing

Be aware: *Some airlines charge fuel surcharges for award bookings on partner airlines, and sometimes taxes are paid separately as they apply*

Cheapest Airfares to Get There

Short Stay Airfares
Air Tahiti Nui offers this extra special all-year-round for trips from LA to Papeete. Only a few seats (usually about 14) on each flight are given to this best possible airfare, so get in early. It can only be used for stays of 5 nights or less. The short stay allowed by a "Short Stay" fare doesn't make it possible to visit more than one island in Tahiti. But if your finances and time are limited, it could be your chance to get to Bora Bora!

If you want to surprise someone with a sensational, short, sweet getaway, this option transports you both to Tahiti for an exceptional price. Accommodation, and an excursion, can easily be packaged into the deal. This is just long enough to experience the delights of Bora Bora.

- You can book **the 'red eye' flight out of L.A.** to arrive early the next morning in Papeete. Then by changing planes for the half hour inter-island flight to Bora Bora, and flying straight on, you enjoy 5 nights and 6 days on Bora Bora.

- Or the **afternoon flight from L.A.** to Tahiti lands you in Papeete late that same night. This means that you must stay overnight in Papeete before taking the inter-island flight to Bora Bora. That gives four nights on Bora Bora.

Low Season Specials

Low season airfares can be *half the price of high season*. Airlines are more likely to have sales for airfares outside of peak season. Avoid the months of June, July, and August, and you will find a much better priced fare.

"Ia Orana" Airfare

This discounted, low season airfare is offered by Air Tahiti Nui twice each year. First in low season from *mid-January to the end of March*, and later on from the *beginning of December to mid-December*. Only 7 seats per flight are eligible for this ticket. You must stay 9 nights or less to be eligible.

Family Deals

Kids Fly Free

The Kids Fly Free fare is also available all year long. It means that for every one adult ticket purchased, one child may fly for free. Only a few seats are available in this category, on each flight, so purchase in advance.

Be Aware: *The taxes still need to be paid so add those into the equation.*

Half Price Luxury

Are you one of those folk who has access to money and are reading this because you love the feeling of getting the most value when spending it? Here's an enviable opportunity that will also mean that you arrive in style and refreshed.

Anytime you buy a (qualifying) Business or First Class ticket for international air travel using your Platinum Card or Business Platinum Card you are entitled to a free ticket for a companion traveler. The seats are super for sleeping and the savings are incredible. To be eligible, the purchase *must be transacted through the American Express Travel* service.

Over 20 airlines participate in this incredible offer. The main ones of interest for those traveling to Tahiti are Air France, which offers this deal for purchase of first *and* business class fares; and Air New Zealand, which is eligible for business class passengers only.

There is no limit to the number of Companion Tickets cardholders are eligible for in the program, and there are no blackout dates. If you can buy a ticket on an available flight and there is space, you are entitled to a Companion Ticket. But only refundable tickets are eligible for these Companion Tickets.

The Platinum American Express Card has no Foreign Transaction Fees, so it also fits into our criteria for a worthwhile credit card to have for traveling.

Be Aware: *The "free" companion tickets are also subject to taxes and fees ranging from $50-$500, a security fee of up to $10, and airline fuel surcharges.*

Make Tahiti a Stopover

Tahiti is an off-the-radar kind of place. So most people wouldn't realize that French Polynesia's international airline frequently offers special stopover deals for passengers flying to Sydney or Auckland. If you intend traveling through the Pacific between Australia or New Zealand and America; watch out for Air Tahiti Nui's offers, or ask your travel agent about this stopover.

Tahiti can also be a stopover when traveling between Australia and South America. LATAM flies between the two continents with 2 interesting stopovers in Tahiti and Easter Island. Even if you don't have enough time or money to go all the way to Bora Bora, we highly recommend a short stopover on Moorea. Simply catch the fast ferry across from Papeete.

Take the Red Eye Flight?

Most flights arrive in Tahiti either very late at night, or during the morning. If you choose a flight that lands in the morning, you will be able to continue straight on to Bora Bora. Taking the "red eye" means you avoid paying for a night of accommodation on the main island of Tahiti. You don't even get full use your hotel as some night flights only land at 1am!

There is much debate about whether it's best to stay the night on arrival in Papeete, or to keep traveling straight through by taking the next inter-island flight after arriving in the morning. Some people prefer to take the night flight and sleep on the plane. Then they arrive in Tahiti in the morning; ready to visit the Papeete market place, or continue on to their inter-island flight. If cost is an issue to you, avoid the extra night of accommodation by arriving on a day flight.

It seems human ingenuity knows no bounds when the motivation is high enough! A (quite respectable) friend of ours traveled to Tahiti on a backpacker's budget to go surfing. He had a roll-up camping mat in his board bag and pulled it out to sleep on, in the airport, after his late arriving flight. He awoke in the morning to have a Tahitian host hang a 'welcome' flower lei around his neck.
Savings $250

Be Aware: *If you can't sleep on airplane flights don't take the red eye flight. It's no use arriving on the world's most beautiful island feeling miserable. It will be one of the most memorable moments of your life!*

Save on Inter-island flights

Cheaper Air Tahiti Flights
The first tip is simple. Book *return* flights from Tahiti to Bora Bora to save up to 20% on the cost of two one-way fares.

The second tip requires skill. It's only possible if you are computer smart, or befriend someone who is. Air Tahiti offers cheaper fares for flights purchased and issued in French Polynesia. If you're able to change the website to the *local* version, you could potentially save tens or hundreds of euros by a click on the button. The Bora Bora pass sold on AirTahiti.com & AirTahiti.fr for 47.000 XPF can be purchased on AirTahiti.pf for 41.700 XPF (50 EUR discount) and is not more expensive during high season. *Savings: $160*

See More Islands for Only A few More Dollars...

If you're considering visiting more than one island (on the same vacation) you can save money by selecting the appropriate Air Tahiti Island Hopper Pass. An Airpass is usually cheaper than buying individual tickets to each island, but not always. I suggest that you check the price for doing it both ways.

These discounted tickets even allow you to discover islands in the distant archipelagos of French Polynesia for an attractive price. There are **two extension options** which, in conjunction with a pass, enable you to visit the **Austral Islands** or part of the **Marquesas Islands** as well.

The Airpass ticket is confirmed, not stand-by. However, you are not permitted to make changes once you begin your journey, as you may on individual tickets.

Be aware: *missing one flight will void the rest of the pass. Be careful about your dates and times when booking.*

Make sure the Airpass your travel agent offers you is the right one. I once received a quote from an agent for a trip which also included the Rangiroa pass option. But we were only going to the Society Islands and the Bora pass would have sufficed. (Of course, if you choose a reputable Tahiti agent such oversights should not occur.)

The price you find online may be the same as, or cheaper than, the one offered by an agent. In that case, check whether the higher prices offered by the agent factor in ground transport on each island, and also "meet-and-greet" fees (which often include a welcome lei). If not, you can book directly with Air Tahiti.

I once used Air Tahiti's website to price out a multi-leg trip that included 4 flights over the course of 3 weeks. I got a very nice price so I booked it online. The process consisted of Air Tahiti confirming the reservation via email, and then advising me that a payment link (via Secure-Server) would be coming soon. The link arrived within 24 hours. I paid, and within hours received an E-ticket and all necessary information, via an email.

Air Tahiti Passes that Include Bora Bora:
Bora Pass (YD215) Moorea, Bora Bora, Huahine, Raiatea/Tahaa, Maupiti
Bora Tuamotu (YD213) Moorea, Bora Bora, Huahine, Raiatea/Tahaa, Maupiti, Rangiroa, Fakarava, Tikehau.

These can be bought online through Air Tahiti's website, or through an agent. At the moment, the Bora Pass is selling for $393.90. When you consider that return flights to Bora Bora cost $414 (during high season) the savings on the extra flights are almost as awesome as the views you will encounter.

Logistics of Air Passes:
- Returning to Tahiti while using the pass is not permitted
- They start and end in Tahiti or Moorea
- You don't have to visit *all* the islands included in the pass
- You can only visit an island once on the same pass
- Maximum length of trip is 28 days from start date, including extensions
- You can buy one or two extensions; to visit the far out Austral or Marquesas Islands, which you can fly and visit before or after using the multi-island pass; extensions must be bought through a travel agent.

Changes & Reimbursement
Air Tahiti has *very generous policies* around changes and reimbursement:
- Time or date changes, but not to itinerary - *no cost*
- Changes to itinerary - 17 EUR
- Reimbursement prior to arrival in French Polynesia - 17 EUR/direction (max. 67 EUR/passenger)
- Reimbursement after arriving in French Polynesia - 50% of ticket price

- Reimbursement after using a portion of the pass - no refund.

The prices of these passes do not fluctuate depending on supply and demand as we are accustomed to with other airlines. Flights between the islands have a fixed price, and providing there is a seat available, you may book the flight.

You must book through a travel agent if:

- *you intend traveling with 100lbs (46k) or more.*
- *You want to start your pass in Moorea.*

If You're Already in Tahiti You Can Purchase:

Cards de Réduction
These can only be purchased at Air Tahiti's down-town Papeete office located at the corner of Rue Marechel Foch and Rue Edouard Ahnne. It's closed on Sunday. Identification and one photo must be shown. When you purchase inter-island tickets while in Tahiti check what your baggage allowance will be. (Lockers are available at the airport.) Travelers under 25 can buy a Carte Jeune. Those over 59 a Carte Marama.

They cost CFP 1,000. These cards give discounts of up to 50%. Full discounts only apply to off-peak flights to Bora Bora and other islands.

Family Cards de Réduction
Family cards cost CFP 2,000. These cards give a 50% reduction for parents and 75% for children under 12 years. Full discount is only given for off-peak flights to Bora Bora and other islands.

Enjoy a 'Free' Scenic Flight!

Try to get to the airport early enough to be towards the front of the queue for boarding. Seating on inter-island flights to Bora Bora is open seating. So the best side of the plane for views is available to the first people who board the plane.

After you enter the plane from the rear, take a seat on the left-hand side as you walk down the aisle. This side of the plane will have the best view, of the most beautiful island in the world, as you approach Bora Bora Airport. Many people know this, so...if it's important to you, get to the airport early.

Disclaimer: Occasionally the wind is blowing from the wrong direction for the pilot to come straight in and land. Instead he must approach from the other side, and the folk on the right of the plane have the best view. Check the forecast before leaving; or ask a crew member, before boarding; which direction the landing is expected to be from.

Savings: $800 for not having to take a 15-minute helicopter tour to get an indelible photograph of the priceless bird's eye view!

Be aware: *Unclaimed seats are usually given to stand-by passengers 20 minutes before a flight. No-shows are charged CFP 4,000 to make a new reservation.*

Cancellation Costs

- If you cancel at least 24 hours before your flight to Bora Bora the fee is CFP 1,000.
- For cancellation with less than 24 hours notice, the fee is CFP 4,000. To make sure it is done, if you are already in Tahiti, cancel in person and have your flight coupon amended.

Air Tahiti struggles to make a profit flying small planes very long distances between islands. It's really a public service, and they need to fill every seat. Hence the strict policy for discouraging "no-shows". If your plans change do the right thing by informing them ahead of time so that you don't waste money.

Be Aware: *Air Tahiti planes can leave early! It's called "island time". Show up early for your inter-flights or you may lose precious vacation time as well as money.*

Another Reason to Use a Preferred Specialist Travel Agent!

We know that misunderstandings between Air Tahiti and regular travel agents in other parts of the world are common. So we advise folk that if their bookings were made from abroad, they confirm their inter-island flights, plus any other Bora Bora travel arrangements, as soon as they arrive in Papeete. A hotel concierge will make the call for you.

But why not select an agent you can trust to be reliable! It's like an insurance policy to have a (fluent in French and English) travel agent's phone number (in the same time zone) so that you can get anything easily sorted out.

Take the Free Airport Ferry

Although the Bora Bora resorts will offer you boat transportation to and from the airport motu (at a high price) there is a complementary option that comes with your air ticket. All you have to do is go outside to the dock and take the next Air Tahiti shuttle boat to Vaitape village. Catch a taxi to your accommodation from there. Unless you're staying at a pension which offers to pick you up from the boat dock at Vaitape.

If you are staying at a resort on a motu, you'll probably be forced to pay the resort's private shuttle fee; or you would have to take a boat, taxi, and another boat; to get to your resort. The extra time and hassle for a little less money spent may not be the best way to arrive in paradise.

The exception is if you are staying at the Conrad Nui. Then you can easily wait on the Vaitape wharf for the resort's next (very regular) shuttle boat and catch it back to check in at reception, which is on the same pontoon where the boat will arrive. Payment is only required when you catch this shuttle in the opposite direction, over to Bora Bora's main island.
Savings: $250 on transfers

Cheaper than Flying?

There is another (twice weekly) option for traveling from Papeete to Bora Bora which is cheaper and makes it possible for those who wish to stop off at more Society islands. It's for the time-rich and dollar-poor, or those turned on by adventure! The **Hawaiki Nui Ferry** sets out from Papeete on

Wednesday's and Fridays, at about 4pm, and arrives at Bora Bora wharf about 10am next morning. The route is reversed the following morning, when Hawaiki heads back to Papeete.

It's basically a cargo boat so not designed with comfort as a priority, but it does have several available cabins with berths. At the moment, the cost for a regular seat is 2000 CFP per adult and 5,800 CFP for a berth.

Adhere to the Luggage Allowance

When packing for Tahiti the adage "less is more" is most appropriate! On inter-island flights (e.g. between Papeete and Bora Bora) the per person weight limits are 23 kg (50lb) for check-in luggage, and 5kg (11 lb) as carry on. Due to safety regulations on small Air Tahiti aircraft these are taken seriously. You *won't* be able to talk your way round them.

Taking More than Your Allowance?

Pay the excess baggage charges for the entire trip when you check-in at Tahiti or Moorea. This makes it possible to take advantage of Air Tahiti's special excess baggage rates:

- "One-island Return Trip" to Bora Bora is Euro 2.60 per kilo of surplus weight.
- A "Multi-islands" for flying to 2 islands including Bora Bora is Euro 3.60 per kilo of surplus weight.
- A "Multi-islands" for flying to more than 2 islands, including Bora Bora is Euro 5.10 per kilo of surplus weight.

(Note that these rates were at time of writing, and the actual cost will fluctuate with daily changes in your currency. Euro 2.60 currently converts to USD$2.88.)

It's important to understand that Air Tahiti operates low-capacity aircraft. The holds of their planes are tiny compared to those of aircraft used for international flights, and baggage is not containerized. As a result, heavy or bulky luggage requires special handling. Calculate (before you go) how much any unusual items will cost to take, so you can decide if they're worth it.

Pack Wisely

You will save lots of dollars simply by ensuring that you bring everything you need from home. Usually when I'm heading off traveling I think that it doesn't matter what I've forgotten, providing I have my passport, credit card, and toothbrush. But not when the destination is Bora Bora! To avoid wasting money on items you already have, or spending more than the same thing would cost you back home, take advantage of our years of experience in traveling at different times of the year.

- Dress is casual simplicity, even at 5 star resorts. This is not just the most *beautiful* place on earth, it's also the most *relaxing*. Tahiti has very warm weather (most days of the year) so you usually just need **light summer cottons**, except for in the air-conditioned bar or dining room in the evening, if you feel the cold.

- I learnt the value of having a lightweight **wind and waterproof jacket** on hand during my first Tahiti travel (when I neglected to pack one). You'll be especially grateful for it during Bora Bora winter months of July and August, when the trade winds blow. The actual temperatures are pleasant, but it can be windy (adding a chill factor) and you'll want to keep protection handy.

- If you're going in the summer months of January and February, we strongly suggest you take 2 (one for backup while the other is drying) sets of **sweater and long pants**, even if you don't end up needing them. Summer is the wet season. We were there in January when a hurricane passed across the Pacific nearby, bringing several overcast days, with intermittent showers. What a surprise we got because no one had told us that Tahiti can be cold! Honeymooners were walking around swaddled in towels. Most resorts have some of their eating places partly open (i.e. no walls) to let in the views, which also lets in the wind. A sweater became so priceless we considered negotiating to purchase one from staff. They were the only folk on the island who were prepared. Even on cloudy days the lagoon still astounded us with its bright blue hues. But it was challenging going outside while shivering in skimpy clothes.

- Bring **flip flops and simple sandals**. Leaving your expensive leather shoes or sandals at home could save hundreds of dollars in replacing them later. You're off to a tropical island where you may be surprised by a (usually) light rain-shower, when you least expect. It's a time to relax rather than be concerned about wading in water with your favorite precious pumps. This is not a concrete jungle, it's the real thing! Much of the time you will be walking on sand, or wooden board walks, with gaps where you would lose your heels.

- Take a **practical hat** (with a wide brim) that scrunches up in your bag and un-crunches when you put it on. An inexpensive hat will be your best friend in Tahiti and with all the water activities, it will likely be introduced to the lagoon sometime. Every day may be 'hat day' so you might also want a stylish one for lounging about your resort.

- Remember to bring **sunscreen and mosquito repellant** (for when you're away from the water). Not only will you have your favorite ones, but they cost more to buy in French Polynesia. You will need to be very generous with applying this over yourself (and your sweetheart).

- **Reef shoes** are essential and I'll take a moment to tell you why, lest you think they're for someone else, not you. You're likely to find better fitting, more comfortable, smaller priced ones back home, and won't have to waste vacation time finding some. The motu islands which create the reef surrounding the Bora Bora lagoon are coral. Pieces break off, lie on the lagoon's sandy floor in some places and can even be moved onto the edge of beaches by the current flowing in and out. Sometimes walking along the water's edge of white sandy beaches is more fun with reef shoes because you can forget about watching out for unexpected sharp bits (that have yet to become sand). Wearing reef shoes, when not wearing flippers, also protects your feet if you accidentally stand on a small sea creature that objects to the insult.

- Everybody should take quality **goggles, snorkel and flippers**. If you've never put your head under water in your life, this is the place to get started! The scenery *under* the water can be just as spectacular as the islands above. Some resorts lend goggles, and when you go on an organized excursion, providers have goggles and snorkels available for borrowing. But you will want your own, that are comfortable and don't leak. If you've never used fins/flippers now is the time to discover what an asset they are for gliding easily through the calm, warm lagoon. Buying such items in Tahiti is likely to cost more for lesser quality, and there isn't much choice.

- I also want to highlight the utility of a **waterproof day bag**. You'll be on beaches, in boats (where water may splash over the side or people may get into wet) and may experience a light tropical shower pass over while walking around. On one excursion, all the things in my bag on the boat got wet because it rained while I was having a great time underwater, snorkeling in the lagoon! Bringing a waterproof bag could save you having personal items spoiled, as well as experiencing the discomfort of wet clothes.

- *Pack a **waterproof camera**!* It's not just useful *under* water. It's also handy for taking in a boat, and walking around in the wet. I overlooked buying one for my first trip, and some of the most incredible sights, arranged themselves, right before my eyes. On my second trip I made sure that I had one, hoping to catch some of those first moments on film. But it is impossible to choreograph the sea creatures and recreate the same elements coming together. I had snorkeled in Rangiroa lagoon that first time, in the clearest water, teeming with living things. I saw sharks and manta rays and colorful coral and hundreds of brightly colored fish. The second visit I was armed with a camera, ready to capture the amazing display. But the sky was grey and it had been raining that morning, so the water was murky from run-off. Anyone experiencing the drift snorkel on that day, for the first time, would have had no idea what was around them.

Yes...packing for a Tahiti vacation must reflect that you will be far from stores (as you know them) and getting around often requires a boat ride! Plus (for safety reasons) Air Tahiti staff are trained to strictly enforce baggage allowances for inter-island flights, so only take what you need. *Savings: extra $10 for fold-up hat, $10 for sunscreen, $10 for reef shoes*

Plus you'll have more choice at home and more time to spend enjoying the world's most beautiful island. It's much more fun shopping for pareos or pearls in Tahiti!

Eat, Drink, and Save

When I told my well-traveled dad that I had booked my first trip to Tahiti he raised his eyebrows and commented dryly that "food is expensive there". That rumor still abounds. Don't let this common perception affect *your* vacation fun. Bora Bora food prices *can* be higher than on some other islands in the sun. But over various visits we have learned how to make choices that save hundreds of dollars. By combining these tips you'll have strategies for eating well in Bora Bora, while keeping food costs down.

Slash Your Drinks Bill

Buy Duty Free Alcohol at LAX

To enjoy your favorites for a great price, buy duty free alcohol at LAX before departing for Tahiti. This is easier now that the lower 17 kilo check-in baggage allowance on inter-island flights around French Polynesia has been increased to 23 kilos to match the international weight limit. When returning home you can use the kilos you drank to take back gifts and souvenirs.

Buy Alcohol at a Supermarket in Tahiti

At the sumptuous Carrefour supermarkets in Papeete (where your international flight arrives in French Polynesia) there's a huge range of beverages, for great prices. It includes some unique island flavored choices. So with the inter-island Air Tahiti check-in baggage limit now at 23 kilo, you can stock up before flying to Bora Bora, and knock hundreds off the drink tab at your resort. Just make sure you keep within the weight limit. On inter-island flights you can also put drinks in your 5 kilo (11 lb) of carry-on, as liquid is not a problem.

Buy Alcohol at a Bora Bora Supermarket

Even if you reach your weight allowance when packing, you still have options. There's a variety of great priced wines and beers available at Chin Lee's market, in Bora Bora's main village, Vaitape. Or at the mini-mart on the Circle Island Road between Intercontinental Le Moana and the Sofitel Marara Resort. Shop with the locals. As many discriminating French ex-patriots reside here you can buy fine French wines for less than back home.

Drink at Your Resort's Bar During Happy Hour!

Seize the daily opportunity offered by "2 for 1 drink's hour". Tantalizing Tahiti cocktails taste even more delicious at half price. The same person is expected to consume both, so technically you cannot give the other glass to your honey, although we've had drink waiters automatically serve one to each of us, and not ask us to buy more. If policy prevails, and you both want a drink, you will need to buy a second set for your partner. But you can have double the fun sampling a variety during your stay.
Savings: $280

Make Your Own Drinks

Sip them in the island ambiance on the deck of your bungalow. Fridge, glasses, ice and bucket are provided. If you're accustomed to a glass or two of wine over dinner, enjoy one while soaking in the balmy, evening air, before you leave your villa and after you return. You'll avoid accumulating a hefty bill for non-essentials that will have to be paid on checking out!

Avoid Pricey Water

Hotel water prices are ouchy and, as it's a warm climate, you're likely to drink a lot. Exercising a little independence will save a bundle.
>Bring your own large water bottles and fill them at the hotel's gym.
>Buy water from a local supermarket at a fraction of resort prices.
>If you're staying at one of the Intercontinental hotels, or visiting Matira Beach, there's a handy convenience store (stocking a bit of everything) just outside the gates of Le Moana. It sells water for a fraction of the resort prices.

It's useful to know that Bora Bora's water supply is produced from seawater so it is safe to clean your teeth with it, and drink it if you need to. It does have chlorine added.
Savings: $250

Eat Well, Save Big

Eat Breakfast, Skip Lunch

Some people report that the breakfast buffets are pricey. We're mindful about how we spend our money and have found them good value. They're worth getting up for! We like to begin the day in island time. Lingering over a sumptuous breakfast buffet signifies that we're on vacation, and leaves the "gulp and run" of regular life far behind. Whatever your taste or culture, there's oodles (and noodles) to select from. It'll fill you up for hours. You can eat lightly for lunch, or may not even need lunch at all.

Watch for a resort offering complimentary breakfast deals. When staying at the Intercontinental we've had breakfast included for an attractive price. The 5 star resorts, and the Thalasso (which has four and a half), boast impressive international spreads, presented with French elegance, in island surrounds. If you stay at Le Moana, you can elect to catch the complimentary boat out to the motu sister resort and partake of an even bigger feast than the beautiful one served in the Polynesian atmosphere of the main island resort (for the same money).

Use Hotel Card Status

Do you reside in North America? We've written at length re the benefits of taking out a hotel credit card before you start booking your vacation. At the moment, the Hilton Gold Card rewards holders with $32 per person towards breakfast at the Bora Bora Nui or Hilton Moorea resort, once you achieve Elite Status. This will save about $500 dollars during a week's vacation for two. Not to be outdone, Le Meridien is rewarding Starwood Preferred Guests with 20% off all resort dining. Check for the rewards to be reaped (and eaten).

When NOT to Buy the Full Meal Plan

Many people ask us how to get an all-inclusive vacation. The closest way of doing that at Bora Bora resorts is to buy their meal plan.
But the resorts are ensuring that they cover all expenses when they price their prepaid meal plans. It seems that to decide what to charge for a meal voucher, they pick the most expensive appetizer, entree, and dessert, on

their menu, and add a (service) fee. If you are not a big eater and skip a course, share a plate, or can't eat everything served up; you've paid too much.

We've discovered that we don't need to purchase the *full* meal plan. We like to get out and eat at other resorts and unique_restaurants around the island. Because of the French influence there's excellent cuisine to be found. We recommend the gastronomic adventure at La Villa Mahana, also known as "seven tables". But it would be hard to justify such an extravagant night out, if already paying full price for dinner at a resort.

We also_visit small cafes and shop with the locals for the_best food prices. Getting around Bora Bora is unlike navigating your way around anywhere else you have been. Look out for the section below with instructions for how to best approach it.

However, *if a great package which includes a meal deal comes along, grab it*. Your vacation will be extra relaxing if you don't need to leave the resort to eat. We once stayed 7 nights, with the full meal plan thrown in, for less than the accommodation would have usually cost. We snapped up that incredible offer the moment we saw it, paid up front, and could book the dates later, after deciding when to go.

Be Aware of the * on the Menu!

Even if you buy the meal plan, Bora Bora resort dining usually includes specialty dishes. They're marked with an * on the menu, and incur a surcharge if you order them. You sit down to dinner (after a superb day on the lagoon) glance at the menu, salivate at the notion of a gourmet veal dish, notice it has an asterisk with an extra $7 surcharge, and be seduced into thinking, "what the heck, I'm on vacation"! The next night you'll probably find that what you want most on the menu, also has an asterisk. If two of you think like that, there'll be an extra $100, or more, on your bill when you leave. How do I know? It happened to me.

Eat Local Produce

If you want the most for your money when selecting what to eat, choose dishes with local ingredients. On this fantasy island, in the middle of the

Pacific Ocean, bounty from the sea is a good option. It's usually tasty and succulent, and gives better value than meat that has traveled from Europe or New Zealand. Polynesian-style dishes often include seafood. We have found that if stuck for a lunch choice we can always count on "poisson cru", which is offered on many menus. It's well priced, fresh and delicious.

Feel Good About *Not* Tipping!

If you're serious about saving money while on vacation in Bora Bora get your head around the fact that tipping is *not* customary in French Polynesia. A *20% tipping amount is already included* in the meal price, along with tax. It's tricky for those who come from a tipping culture (where the waiter would glare) but you really can feel fine leaving your table without giving a tip. Save that yummy money for happy hour!

Skip the Polynesian Banquet Fee

Most resorts hold a weekly Polynesian banquet night. Guests who have bought the meal plan may choose to pay a surcharge (on top of their meal costing) to feast on **dishes prepared by traditional methods**. If your meals have not been included in your hotel booking, you are asked to pay the full price to participate, and it's not cheap.

This event includes a **colorful performance of vibrant Tahitian dancing,** in dazzling costumes. You *must* see one of these engaging shows whilst in Tahiti. We enlarge on how to view this, without incurring the hefty expense. However, before setting your hotel dates, check (with an email or phone call) that the advertised night for this event, is still correct, as timetables can change periodically. Prevent missing one if you're not staying 7 nights at the same resort.

Some **resorts also feature Polynesian mammas demonstrating their traditional crafts** on this special night. But don't assume you'll be missing out on a unique cultural experience if you choose not to book for the banquet. It's (usually) unnecessary to pay for this because the exhibition is held in a public area of the resort so guests are free to watch. Plus, if you check with the activities desk on arrival you'll find that on several days there's some kind of free cultural activity on offer, at a certain time and place.

We've never had to pay a premium, to participate in this special evening, but have enjoyed a colorful dancing show, many times. We just happened to be eating in eye-sight. Or hotel staff invited us to come and watch, even though we had not booked for the banquet. It's in their interests for you to act as an ambassador by taking home colorful scenes reflecting that Polynesian culture is alive and well. You can sit at the bar and have a snack and a drink, if you want. Feel fine to stand on the side and take photographs and videos if you wish. The manager wants you to have a wonderful time.

If you're considering a cruise this is one more way to automatically save dollars. **Each Tahiti itinerary includes a Polynesian night extravaganza** which is included in the cost. It's timed for while the ship is actually docked at a wharf. This is only possible at Raiatea or Papeete as the other islands are surrounded by reefs, and the lagoons are too shallow to bring a ship safely into shore. At other islands ships anchor in deeper water offshore, so the Polynesian entertainers would have to be ferried to and fro by small tender boat.

You don't need to buy the banquet as there are other **cheaper opportunities for tasting traditional food**. Each resort has some Polynesian dishes as on menus. The Nui even has a dedicated Polynesian restaurant in a section of its vast restaurant-bar building, which only opens in the evenings. The bountiful servings of island food are presented as a fantastic visual feast. They're delicious, well priced, and we had very attentive service. The experience was so enjoyable that we ate there on three nights during our week's stay. If you choose to stay at the Nui, book at the front desk, soon after arrival, to be sure of placements, as there's a limited number of seats.

However, *there is an exception.* Be warned that on one night of the year you may get caught without a choice! Virtually every resort in Bora Bora expects you to pay for this grand event, if you're their houseguest on New

Year's Eve! Only one hotel did not have this rule when I last enquired, and that was Le Maitai, which we don't actually class as a resort, because the only form of luxury bestowed there is the awesome view.

If you're present for New Year's Eve festivities *have your glass topped up frequently with the fantastic French wines* that flow freely. You'll forget that you're paying between $100 and $200 dollars per person. Decorative, masks, hats and playthings are handed out to everyone. Celebration is in the air! Some resorts provide a fireworks display to summon in the new year. But you don't have to stay at one of those to see shooting stars. The December we were vacationing in Bora Bora for New year we enjoyed the Four Seasons and the Intercontinental displays, watching from the pontoon of our own resort, while blowing toy trumpets.

If you're staying in Pension type accommodation, talk with your host about where the most superb vantage point will be. Those staying in the Vaitape area of the island don't even have to find a position to watch a resort show because there is a special event held near the Vaitape wharf. A grandstand is erected and there's a traditional show, followed by fireworks. This gives islanders a festive night.

Catch the Polynesian Dance Show!

Fortunately, for both locals and travelers, Tahitian dance survived the western missionary influence which declared all "pagan" traditions taboo. It's now the most valued part of Polynesian culture and islanders take exceptional pride in this joyful, expressive art-form.

Where to Go for the Best Show

The **Intercontinental hotel near the airport** on Tahiti's main island has one of the best Polynesian dance displays in French Polynesia. It showcases dancers from Les Grands Ballets de Tahiti. This may be one more reason to stay at an Intercontinental on Bora Bora. Because if you make this choice, a Tahiti specialist may be able to get you a very special price (or even a free night) for accommodation in Papeete, when you arrive or depart.

Each of the 3 Bora Bora villages has its own awesome dance team. They rehearse frequently to compete in the Heiva Festival during July, and entertain at resorts, so you might hear the beat of the drums while exploring the island. Which Bora Bora resort has the best one? It doesn't matter which hotel you see a show at, as the dance teams rotate. We've viewed a show at the humble Maitai which was as good as elsewhere.

On **Moorea**, one of the cultural attractions, the **Tiki Village**, has a Polynesian buffet (for just under $100) but the standard of the food is average. However, the accompanying traditional dance show is recognized as the best on the island.

Know the Places for Casual Eating

The actual price of food at Tahiti resorts is comparable to the better resorts in Hawaii. But the main difference in Bora Bora is that *there are only a few choices for casual dining*. Some of these are a little obscure and you have to know about them, plus *how to get around* the island, if you want a wider choice of places to eat. When staying out on a motu resort there are logistics like boat transfers and taxis involved. There are also time limitations in their operating hours to be aware of.

Look for a Cheaper Island-style LUNCH

Aloe Cafe

Aloe Cafe is in the Pahia Center at Vaitape Village, diagonally across the road from the church, Eglise Evangelique Temple. It's a pastry shop, and snack restaurant, excelling in delicious pastries.

The menu has a wide selection of meals and snacks at reasonable prices. Everything from traditional **poisson cru to crepes, paninis, salads, kabobs, pizza, hamburgers, and tempting ice-cream sundaes**. It's the most popular Bora Bora cafe and locals eat here daily. Drinks include coffee and espresso, teas, a local selection of fresh fruit juices, and beer. Aloe is also a convenient internet cafe, offering internet access from 4

computers, plus printers, scanners, and webcams. Prices (subject to change) are: 400 XPF/$4.30 for 10 minutes, 1,000 XPF/$11 for 30 minutes, 1600 XPF/$17 for 60 minutes.
Open Monday to Saturday from 6.30 am-5pm. Cash only. Tel.67.78.88

Le Paradisio
Le Paradisio is in Centre Mautera, a little shopping center on the mountain side of the road, a few minutes walk south of Vaitape Village. This is truly a place to be among locals. It's little known to tourists. The menu is written in French and offers **French and Turkish 'fast' food, along with milkshakes, coffee and beer.**
Le Paradisio is open for breakfast and lunch. Tel. 90.59.83

Snack Matira
Snack Matira (also known as Chez Claude) is an open air snack bar set right beside the lagoon at award winning_Matira Beach, which is one of Bora Bora's top attractions. If you want to have lunch or a snack while visiting this stunning beach you can continue to enjoy the stunning lagoon ambiance while eating here. The roulette style menu offers **grilled steak and fish, burgers, pizzas, salads, omelets, and casse-croûte sandwiches,** plus ice cream and milkshakes.
Snack Matira is open 10am-4pm. Closed Mondays and the Christmas period through to 1st week in January. Cash only. Tel. 67.77.32

Ben's
Ben's is across from Snack Matira, on the mountain side of the road at Matira Beach. Ben Teraitepo, a native of Bora Bora, and his vivacious U.S. wife Robin (who has even made local calls for us) cook and serve meals with a friendly chat.

Their American orientated menu includes **Tex Mex food, cheeseburgers, hot dogs, submarine sandwiches, pizzas, lasagna, spaghetti with a choice of sauces,** plus the mandatory fresh island fish. Dishes are priced from 700 XPF/$7.50 to 1600 XPF/$17.
Ben's is open 8am to 5pm daily. Closed Christmas period through 1st week in January. Cash only.

Eat with the Locals for LUNCH or DINNER

Roulette Matira

Roulette Matira is directly across the road from the entrance to Matira Point and Le Moana Resort, but might be missed unless you're looking out for it. This handy snack bar is a great place to go for tasty food at reasonable prices. Choices include **fresh seafood, a beef dish with rice, a tasty burger, or a quick sandwich**. It's not a mobile roulette (like those you may see in Vaitape or the wharf front in Papeete) but set back from the road in an intriguing garden. Watch out for the original cart which sits at the entrance.

Roulette Matira's quirky outside eating environment is fun, the food is delicious, and the friendly service is offered with enough English and smiles to enable you get what you want. You can eat here for between $10 and $18. It also has bicycle rental.

Roulette Matira advertises open for lunch 11.30-2pm and dinner 6.30-9pm but occasionally they're closed for "island time". (If you get caught out, Fareau Manuia is close by). Cash only. Tel. 67.67.39

Snack Moihere

This basic Polynesian cafe/restaurant, with a thatched roof held up by tree limbs, sits above the main area of Matira beach near Matira Point. When we visited, the decor was jaded, but on the up side, we didn't have to leave the beach, or its incredible views, to eat cheaply, and it's open from sunup to late.

Snack Moihere offers what has now become local-style food, starting with a **continental breakfast**. Lunch becomes **hamburgers, omelets or sandwiches**. A roulette-like dinner menu includes **steak or fish served with fries, hamburgers, chow mein and poisson cru**. Dishes cost 650 XPF/$7 to 2400 XPF/$25.

Snack Moihere is open daily from 6am-9pm. Credit card minimum 2,000XPF. Tel.67.56.46

Fare Manuia

To have a taste of what living on Bora Bora is like, we highly recommend visiting Fare Manuia which offers a friendly atmosphere, good simple food, and non-stop service. You'll meet more locals here than at any other Bora Bora restaurant. They gather on Friday night. The patio out the back has a bar and a swimming pool, which was purchased from the iconic, now closed, Hotel Bora Bora. There's a cocktail of the day for 1.200XPF/$13.

Love pizza? The wood fired pizza oven in the front terrace area offers 28 pizza choices priced from 1.200XPF/$13 to 1.900XFP/$20. The day menu also has **15 different paninis and types of burgers**, all served with fries. A varied dinner menu is a combination of **gastronomic French cuisine and island specialties**. Dishes start at 1.800XPF/$19 and a 3-course menu is 3.900XPF/$41.
Restaurant Fare Manuia is located on the lagoon side just after the turn-off at Point Matira. It's open daily from 11.30am to 10pm. Free pick up for dinner. Tel. 67.68.08 / 72.52.84

La Bounty

La Bounty offers a French menu, in an island décor, with a sand floor. At last visit the building was a little tired but it had an extensive menu featuring delicious sauces. You can have a simple **pizza, a tender beef rib or opt for shrimp, salmon or steak** with a wide choice of sauces.

This is another restaurant frequented by French locals. Our personal experience was that the quality of the food and service depended on how busy the staff was. A large pizza is 1.500XPF/$16 and most entrees/mains cost $30.
La Bounty is located a few minutes north from Point Matira, between Le Maitai and the Sofitel. It's also walking distance from Intercontinental Le Moana. It's open for lunch and dinner. Closed Monday.
Savings: $300+

Buy from the Supermarket

To find a supermarket while getting around in French Polynesia watch out for the sign, 'Magasin'. Purchase snacks and grocery items for eating during the day and save on lunches and breakfasts (if you don't buy a meal plan). You can choose from a range of cold meats, French cheeses (my favorite is the garlic Boursin), fresh salad vegetables, and tropical fruit, to have a very tasty feast for a nice price. Fresh, crunchy baguettes are popular island fare and can be bought for about 60 cents.

When passing through **Papeete** on your way to Bora Bora, try and get to one of the *Carrefour Supermarkets*. They are supermarket sized French delis with an overwhelming display of delicious foods, patisserie treats, and drinks; that delight the eye and taste buds! Many mouth-watering, freshly prepared 'dishes' are arrayed in easy, 'ready to go' packaging. Good luck choosing between them!

You may have to use some playful sign-language, as you'll not find much English there. That's part of the fun! Prices are moderate but before you start stocking up for Bora Bora know how much your bags weigh. (The check-in clerks are trained to be ruthless, on account of the small plane size).

On the main island at **Bora Bora** there are also several small supermarkets. It's easy to stop at one of these lively stores to pick up a convenient, cheap lunch while exploring the main island. We also suggest you buy items to take back to your hotel fridge for snacks.

- *Chin Lee Market* is the busiest place in Vaitape as its frequented by many locals and a few tourists. You'll find it near another popular venue, the church. Chin's also has delicious take-away platters of cooked food for great prices.
- *Tiare Market* is usually bustling with tourists as it's conveniently located between the Maitai and Sofitel, just a few minutes walk north from Matira Point and Intercontinental Le Moana, or south from the Sofitel. It's smaller, but the vast variety of goods stocked on the shelves is surprising.

- **Super U** is further away from the resorts and most other accommodation so you need to go there by car or bicycle. Head north from Vaitape center, on the Circle Island Road, to find it on the right side of the road. This is larger than Chin Lee's and has the very cheapest prices of any store on Bora Bora. It's where the *real* islanders prefer to shop.

Eat Like the Locals

Eat at a roulette
For an authentic Tahitian dining experience, eat at the small roadside "snacks" and roulettes at the side of the road. They offer tasty, inexpensive meals in the great outdoors. Why not do as the locals?

Buy snacks and fresh fruit on the Circle Island Road
As you travel around the island's one main road, look out for small tables set up with fresh fruit or homemade pastries for sale. They're pop-up shops and may be missed as often there won't be a person around to collect money. They rely on an honesty system. You can find treats such as whole bowls filled with freshly picked mangoes for only a couple of dollars per lot. They grow wild and entrepreneurial folk pick them. By purchasing from these stalls, you will be helping islanders, as well as saving lots! Those with cooking facilities can also keep an eye out for fishermen who string up their excess catch-of-the-day for sale.

Bring Snacks from Home

Like Europe, French Polynesia has *no* customs restrictions regarding food. So (unlike if you're coming to strict Australia) it's possible to bring your favorite snacks from home.

Eat Off-Shore

Visiting Bora Bora on a cruise ship is another way to "eat like kings" without paying Tahiti's food prices. It's also the most economical and easiest way to see a selection of pristine islands. Princess Cruises sail around Tahiti with small ships (which means less passengers) to enable them to enter the shallower water in lagoons. During three of these cruises we've found the food to be of a much higher quality than that served up on similar priced cruises (on large ships) in other parts of the world. Especially when the ship has loaded up on supplies in New Zealand!

Shame-free Shopping

In Tahiti, you can have a tiny shopping budget and take home gorgeous souvenirs and gifts that are exquisite and unique. Some of the most precious things we have bought only cost a few dollars.

- *For the very best prices* on **Bora Bora,** shop at the Arts and Crafts Center at Vaitape wharf, and avoid hotel gift shops.
- The vibrant **central market in downtown Papeete** sell souvenirs at *cheaper prices* than in the outer islands where they are made. It's surprising!
- The two **Carrefour supermarkets in Papeete** also stock a variety of competitively priced souvenirs and all kinds of goods, including shelves and shelves of fragrant coconut oil (monoi oil) and tamanu oil products. This is the place to purchase, if you forget to bring something from home.
- Be aware of bargaining practices. Haggling over prices in markets and stores is not usual (or acceptable) behaviour in French Polynesia. But every rule has an exception! When purchasing higher priced pearl jewelry, you *can ask for a discount.*

Shop for Handmade Souvenirs

Buy big on low-priced island pretties. You'll delight family and friends with natural pieces of paradise and have regular reminders of your vacation, without putting a dent in your credit card! You can also feel good because purchasing these ensures that priceless skills are passed on. You're supporting the islanders who make a simple living from their elegant, traditional crafts such as:

Hand Painted Pareos
Buying a pareo is likely to be top of your shopping list once you realize this is Tahiti's national dress. And you'll certainly find them more comfortable than jeans! You can get a little guide book or complimentary pamphlet that shows women how to tie them in numerous ways, to flatter every kind of

figure. But they're for men too. You'll see Polynesian dudes keeping *everything* cool, with this simple garment knotted around their waist.

These lively pieces of cotton fabric are about 2 yards long and one yard wide. There's a colorful choice of designs that are hand painted, airbrushed, or tie-dyed. Check labels to ensure you're not purchasing mass printed rayon from Indonesia or some other place! To get your money's worth, look for a locally hand-printed, cool *cotton* one to enjoy the authentic look, feel, and drape. If you stay at the Sofitel there will be an opportunity (one day of the week) to make one yourself. Or you can drop in to see the island mammas making them, and buy from the source. Some on-land excursions include this stop.

Natural Shell Rings, Bracelets and Necklaces
You can choose from a multitude of delicate or chunky, individual designs. There's no need to keep this jewelry in a safe, or feel guilty about the price tag. It's fun to wear and makes great conversation starters back home.

Woven Hats and Baskets
The dexterous creativity expressed in the design of these everyday items is extraordinary and beautiful. They're light, cool, flexible, and oh so neutral. I don't know my grass hat is on my head and it goes with any of my casual summer gear.

Traditional Tahitian Beauty Products
Coconut oil imbued with tiare or frangipani blossom, known as Monoi oil, makes an uplifting moisturizer, massage oil, hair tonic, *and* mosquito guard. Tiare is a national emblem and you'll be introduced to one of these exquisitely-scented, white flowers as you wait to go through customs on arrival at the international airport. For me it was in the middle of the night, with ukuleles strumming in the background. In that moment, I knew I had come to the most sense-enlivening place on earth. Perfumed coconut oil potions have been used by Tahitians for hundreds of years. Don't leave Tahiti without some!

Browse for Bargains

There's no bustle here (unless it's one of the few days per year that a cruise-ship comes in). Browsing is so relaxing in the little stores around Bora Bora. Some carry individual pieces from local artisans, practical and ornamental, and it's possible to pick up something unique at an attractive price.

- *Maison de la Presse* in Vaitape has a selection of coffee table books on French Polynesia, at lower prices than you'll find at your hotel's shop.
- *Bora Bora Home* in the center of Vaitape has a striking display of Polynesian arts and crafts, jewelry, and home and fashion accessories.
- *Bora Bora Spirit* is worth a visit if you want a T shirt that no one else has back home. Mare Tavner prints a colorful array of nicely cut, high quality cotton ones with a Bora Bora flavor.

Save on Tantalizing Tahitian Pearls

Black pearls have been popular in Paris for years. So due to their rarity in nature, they must be cultured under very specific farming conditions to keep oysters healthy and producing up to 4 subsequent pearls over their lifetime. The crystal clear, warm lagoons of French Polynesia are perfect for this. Thus the world's most prized black pearls are farmed in the lagoons surrounding some islands, and way out in the pristine atolls.

During your vacation, you'll have opportunities to buy them for a much cheaper price than you would pay back home. We think that everyone must take home at least one Tahitian black pearl. (You're probably thinking… but this book is about saving money!) The good news is that everyone can afford a jewel of the ocean, as there are various ways to buy pearls and save.

Why You Can Save Big
1. **Visitors are exempted from paying the 16% VAT** that the French

Polynesian government adds, and is already included in the displayed price of graded pearls which have been made into jewelry. Just make sure the vendor fills out paperwork to show that you are a tourist so that the tax component isn't included when you pay. Hand the form to a customs officer when departing from the Papeete airport. Unless you do this, 16% of the purchase price will be charged to your credit card 6 months later.

2. **Individual pearls are not taxed**, no matter how valuable. So by purchasing those you can avoid the issue of tax. It's likely to cost you less to have a jeweler make them up back home as the price of gold is high in Tahiti.

3. Although perfectly formed and lacquered pearls *are* costly, due to their rarity, and the dedicated team required to produce them, **those not wanting to make a pricey purchase have other choices for buying gems from the lagoon**. These cheaper (but still beautiful ones) are *only available here* because the government has a strict policy that only graded black pearls may be exported.

4. **There are opportunities to buy at the source,** on an actual pearl farm, which means avoiding middlemen and transport.

Options for Buying Pearls:
- You can purchase a single pearl, set on a thin leather band, for just a few dollars. It'll have a lovely luster and its imperfection has been eliminated by a fine etching of something of cultural significance, such as a turtle or a dolphin.
- Look for a single pearl which speaks to you (or a pair), of the grade you can afford, and have them made up simply.
- Gold is quite expensive in French Polynesia (and they only use 18K) so if you desire a gold setting, another way to save is to buy individual pearls and have a jeweler set them back home.
- Lower grade pearls, which are not exactly round, or large, or evenly coated, have an inherent beauty and mystery of their own. They may be strung into a striking bracelet or necklace which

hides flaws (with the holes that are drilled) or features their imperfect shapes.

- If you're coming for a special occasion you may want to seize the (cheaper priced than back home) opportunity to purchase an exclusive piece of eye-catching jewelry which will be a treasured memory for life.

You will only find cheaper, ungraded pearls (but still beautiful) at markets and on stalls.

Guard Your Card Around Lagoon Gems

If your goal is to have a wonderful vacation, while saving in as many ways as you can, you may be clever to stay right out of pearl boutiques. Especially if you have a weakness for beautiful jewelry. Black pearls are such a glamorous symbol of Tahiti that many an innocent tourist (including me) has succumbed to their charm.

However, if you do want to make a purchase, decide how much you can spend, and then look around at several merchants to discover what style you prefer. Learn how to judge their quality. Start at the store in the Papeete airport if you have the time. They have a wide selection and their prices are good. Keep in mind that when you see something that catches your eye, in your price bracket, buy it; as you're unlikely to get back.

'Smarts' for Buying High Quality Pearls

Know what to look for (and what you're looking at). If you've budgeted for buying a special piece of Tahitian jewelry, find out how cultured black pearls are made. You'll get more satisfaction. You're buying miracles of nature, which oysters have produced, with a little intervention from man. French Polynesia adheres to a set of European international standards to determine pricing. But you don't need a jeweler's eye, or special equipment, to know about a pearl. Its qualities are visible with the naked eye.

Know How Tahitian Pearls are Graded

Luster
This means sheen, which describes how light reflects from the pearl's surface. Luster is judged to be: excellent, very good, good, medium, or poor.

Surface perfection
Just viewing the surface with a naked-eye examination allows you to assess smoothness. Look for punctures, scratches, deposits, streaks, or swellings. The natural coating is 'oyster-made' so a flawless surface is rare. While pearls are being 'strung' or mounted, a jeweler takes great care with drilling the holes, so as to erase small imperfections.
When evaluating luster and smoothness, pearls are classed as: Top gem, A grade, B grade, C-grade, D-grade.

Size
A pearl's diameter is measured in millimeters and usually ranges from 8mm to 16mm. This is actually determined by the size of the nucleus (an aragonite bead) that is surgically inserted into the oyster. During the life of an oyster, each time a pearl is carefully removed, a slightly larger one is put back into the cavity. It's critical to keep oysters healthy so they live long, productive lives, creating large pearls that fetch the top prices.

Shape
Pearls are sorted into 7 basic shapes: Round, Semi-round, Drop, Oval, Button, Semi-baroque (uneven, non-symmetrical), and Ringed (called circled). Naturally you'll pay a premium price for perfectly round ones.

Color
This criterion is the most subjective. It really depends on personal taste. Tahitian black pearls are not actually black. They come in a wide variety of hues and tints. You can select from cherry, peacock, pistachio, pink, golden, gray, or white. There's a lot of expensive, perfect, gray ones to be seen and they've been the fashion in France. But the unusual soft colors intrigue me.

Get a Guarantee They Meet Official Standards

One aspect that is not immediately obvious, is how thick the surface (nacre) coating actually is, although the depth of the luster gives a clue. But when buying pearls classed as export quality you can be confident that they meet official standards. These will give a lifetime of pleasure without the disappointment of having the surface lustre wear off; providing you care for them appropriately. In Tahiti they're the *only kind permitted to be sold in actual pearl boutiques* so you can buy with confidence, knowing you won't be cheated.

Shop at Boutiques Reputed for Value & Satisfaction

Tahia has pearl farms in the Tuamotu Atolls, and is reputed for choosing the highest quality black pearls to incorporate in her designs. As a former Miss Tahiti, she's almost a legend for her talent at creating gorgeous jewelry of impeccable taste. It's truly in a class of its own. Her stores feature many of the stunning designs she has won international awards for over the years. To purchase top quality Tahitian black pearls in exquisite designs, at a great price, you can visit her three boutiques in Bora Bora. (There's also one on the waterfront in Papeete.)

One Tahia shop is in Vaitape village and another, grander one, graces the Intercontinental Thalasso Resort. (Four Season's now have one too, but only house guests may go to that resort.) If you want to avoid temptation, leave your credit card in your hotel safe while you explore an Aladdin's cave. It'll open your eyes (or dazzle them) to what makes black pearls so valuable. The service is gracious and informative. Staff happily take out precious pieces and help you try them on. There's a highly professional ambiance, without any snobbishness.

Arc en Ciel stands ahead of the crowd as continuing to earn gratitude for offering great value. If you decide to buy a piece of quality pearl jewelry (since you're visiting Treasure Island) you'll have a wide choice here, at very competitive prices. Wendy, the Polynesian owner prides herself as a pearl expert and personally selects all the pearls on show. She has a team of friendly islanders to assist you.

You'd not find this boutique unless you know about it, as it's off the beaten track. Simply phone (689) 71 98 89 to arrange a free pick-up. Just decide how much you *can spend wisely* before you go because temptation abounds! This outing is a fantastic free thing to do in wet weather.

Buy at a Pearl Farm

From the east side of Bora Bora, the isle of Le Tah'aa is visible on the horizon. In its pristine lagoon there's a family pearl farm named Champon which produces some of the most entrancing shades of pearls in all of French Polynesia. In the Resources section, we explain how to visit from Bora Bora.

I bought my first pearl while visiting a farm at Rangiroa (on a Tahiti cruise). We observed the technicians grafting oysters and had the joy of removing large, shiny pearls from oysters who had done their last work. There was a huge display in the farm store but I easily spotted the one with my name. It shimmered with all the colors of the Bora Bora lagoon. The jeweler attached a loop so I that I can wear it as a pendant, which I treasure. My mamma found 2 almost identical small pearls which were made into earrings, on the spot. We each spent about $300. If you're planning to visit more than one island, Rangiroa is an excellent choice. It's the closest atoll and attractions include a pristine lagoon with a pearl farm, superb drift snorkeling, and the only winery in all of French Polynesia.

Be aware: *If you buy graded pearl jewelry ensure you have your receipt handy when you are departing at the airport, to be entitled to your credit.*

To Do, or Not to Do...Activities and Excursions

There's a lot on offer in Paradise. Jet skiing. Parasailing. Submarine rides. Helmet diving. Motu picnics. Snorkeling with sharks. Cruising at sunset. The list goes on! Our aim here is to help you narrow down what to do to have a wonderful time, without frittering away dollars.

Only Take the "Must Do" Tours

What makes Bora Bora so loved is the lagoon. Get out and enjoy it. If you only take one tour, go on a boat that circles around the main island showing sensational views across the water to every angle of Bora Bora and its towering peaks. A lagoon tour is a must! Even if you don't like to get wet (which may change when you feel its temperature) it's the only way to fully appreciate the awesome beauty that has travel magazines gushing and declaring this "world's number one island", year after year.

The most interesting Circle Island Tours offer opportunities to safely **pat stingrays and view shy reef sharks**. They also include **snorkeling stops at coral gardens** which have more abundant marine life than you can see at most Bora Bora resorts. It might cost a little more but we highly recommend selecting one that includes a **picnic stop on a pristine white-sand motu**.

For us the most memorable moments have been when prevailing conditions allowed the tour guide to take the little outrigger canoe outside the reef to the deep ocean. Wearing goggles, we could see clearly through that silky, transparent, royal-blue water. Lemon tipped sharks were swimming by beneath us, and way-down deep in the distance we could see divers following sharks along the sandy floor. Ask your guide if it's possible to do this.

If you want a second excursion, and are up for noisy action, our favorite travel agent recommends taking a **jet-ski ride tour** which leads you right around the main island. You'll get more for your money by booking one which also includes a thrilling ATV ride across a sandy motu.

Pay Less for Tours & Get More for Your $$

To save on tours *book your own* with the best providers. A tour will cost about 20% more if you ask your resort to arrange it, as they put a commission fee on top. And usually they only patronize certain providers. We suggest that you *book in advance* so that the one you want won't be sold out. Our website has detailed descriptions of the diverse tours on offer. If you're buying a vacation package through a trusted Tahiti travel agent, it should include a lagoon tour at a good price.

Private tours are very expensive so thankfully there's no need to splurge on one. Just *check that you're booking for a tour in a Tahitian outrigger canoe.* That gives everyone a front row ticket to the lagoon and there's only about a dozen people on board. Avoid being a sardine in a large boat with many rows of seats. This is the world's most beautiful lagoon!

We highly recommend **Lagoon Service**; which is co-owned by an entertaining islander (who has a tiny motu in the lagoon) and a local Frenchman. You can rely on Marona, and the friendly islanders he has trained, to treat you to similar exciting experiences as those described above.

Be aware: *Purchasing ahead of time means that you will be able to get your preferred tour company. See our website for the lowdown on what's available. On the rare occasion that excursions cannot be done because of weather, they are rescheduled for another day. Book for early in your stay.*

Create Your Own

If you don't want to part with money for a private tour, and don't want to be shown around in a group, here's another option which we have taken twice. **Hire a motorboat from La Plage** (see the Resources section for contact details) and enjoy an independent lagoon adventure, which enables you to go where you want at leisure. You don't need a boat licence or any special experience, just a spirit of adventure. You'll be given a detailed map of what you must know around the lagoon, including what beaches you are entitled to go to, and where you may anchor.

You can: tie the boat to a buoy at the popular Aquarium for a snorkeling stop; anchor over shallow water and coat yourself with a mineral mud mask; and pull into a white sand beach on a motu. We hauled our craft onto a sandy motu beach and enjoyed strolling along the water's edge in the appropriate direction to catch the current for an awesome drift snorkel back to the boat. Along the way we sighted a wide variety of lagoon life, including a group of rare eagle rays.

Be on Vacation

On this idyllic island, *there's nothing you have to do outside your resort.* Each Bora Bora resort is set on a picture-postcard beach and offers complimentary activities. You can leave the "do, do, do," at home. This is the place to *be*. Soaking in the perfect blue lagoon, white-sand, palm-tree ambiance is both exhilarating and refreshing. Don't feel compelled to spend an extra cent. Although it might cost more to stay at a resort, there are many intrinsic savings.

As stated previously, a lagoon tour, with a shark and ray experience, plus snorkeling stops, *is* a *must*. But apart from that you don't need to do anything at all to have an amazing vacation. Don't over-schedule outings and excursions.

Select a Resort with Freebies

Having everything included, and just a few steps from your thatched-roof bungalow, saves spending money on things to do, and gives more high quality vacation time! We emphasize the wisdom of choosing your accommodation for its beach and activities.

Even if you're visiting Bora Bora on a *tiny* budget, go for a great deal on a garden villa at one of the lower priced resorts. By staying in a resort you'll enjoy so many extras for your money.

After checking in on your first day, visit the beach boy and make a note of times and places to go for the activities you want to participate in. Otherwise at the end of your stay you'll find you've missed some experiences.

Resorts Offer a Wide Range of Complimentary Activities:

1. **Kayaking and Outrigger Canoes** – Paddle around the calm lagoon, from your resort's beach, anytime, without having to make arrangements or think what it will cost.

2. **Snorkeling** – Bring your own snorkeling gear or use the complimentary equipment provided at the resorts. The Conrad Nui and the Sofitel Private Island offer the best opportunities for free snorkeling. Some resorts provide snorkeling excursions, with a biologist pointing out marine life during a guided tour.

3. **Paddle Boarding** – There's no better place in the world to learn this watersport than on the calm Bora Bora lagoon. Some resorts have been quick to make paddle boards available for guests so take this perfect free opportunity to learn. I acquired my paddle boarding legs at the Nui, which has loads of water equipment.

4. **Hobie Cat Cruise** – Most resorts have one of these colorful craft and treat guests to a complimentary ride around the lagoon, with a sailor in charge. As there's only one, book for this popular activity as soon as you've checked in.

5. **Work Out** – You're likely to have the resort's gym to yourself. So enjoy the best view and the purest Pacific Ocean air while you work out in heaven.

6. **Cultural Activities** – Most resorts have a daily activity to show off island traditions. To catch demonstrations on how to tie your pareo, or weave a traditional basket, you have to find out what day, time, and location it's on.

Free Activities Unique to Specific Resorts:

Swim with stingrays at Intercontinental Thalasso
Each day at the Intercontinental Thalasso a beach boy attracts the super friendly stingrays by feeding them in shallow water on the beach. This is superb viewing right from a sun-lounge. But you're also welcome to go in and swim with the rays if you wish.

Turtle Sanctuary Tour at Le Meridien
Le Meridien guests have a large inner lagoon, harboring tropical fish and turtles. Each morning there's a turtle feeding and a talk by a marine biologist. I was fascinated to hear that the turtles' naturally built-in GPS navigates them thousands of miles back to their own birthplace, to give birth to their young. You can also book to swim with the turtles.

Cool Kid's Club at Four Seasons
Would you like to save child care fees on a holiday that'll enthrall *every* member of the family? This value-packed bonus treats children and teens to all day complimentary activities in dedicated kid's areas where they don't have to be bothered by parents and such.

Guided snorkeling tours
The Conrad Nui is engaged in a special project to restore coral and offers a guided snorkeling tour off its beach. Marine biologists provide snorkeling tours in the lagoonariums at the St Regis and Four Seasons Resorts.
Self-paddle to the Aquarium

Bora Bora's most popular coral garden lies just off the back of the Sofitel Private Island. Guests can use canoes and kayaks to row around for their own leisurely snorkeling expeditions. If you are strong and adventurous this can also be done from Le Maitai, but you will have to paddle further and through stronger currents.

Excursions for Cruisers

If you decide to see Bora Bora by cruise ship, you'll save lots on accommodation, meals, and travel; and there's one more way to keep dollars in your own pocket. The cruise lines add at least 20% to the cost of a tour, and they choose providers who can take the largest number of passengers. We've taken a few cruises and chatted with fellow travelers, at the end of the day, over dinner. Sometimes passengers who booked through the ship reported logistical problems that simply should not have occurred. So paying extra doesn't guarantee that your "once in a lifetime" experience will be perfect.

On shore day, it's easy to get off the ship in the morning and buy excursions on the Vaitape dock. (They even accept U.S dollars.) A variety of the main tour providers will have representatives set up on the wharf, close by to where the ship's tender-boat puts passengers ashore. There'll be colorful posters and information on all types of tours that are available. You'll be able to speak with a local, and get a clear idea of what your experience will be, before you choose. But, to save time on the day, or to get a particular tour provider, we recommend that you *book your excursions, yourself, before leaving for a cruise vacation.*

If you book your holiday on Tahiti's very own cruise ship, **Paul Gauguin**, excursions are included in the fare. *A Paul Gauguin cruise is a 100% all-inclusive Tahiti vacation.*

Find Free Things to Do

There are so many fabulous free things to do in Bora Bora (starting with opening your eyes) that you wouldn't actually need to spend a cent other than paying for your resort. These can be done from a hotel stay or a cruise:

1. Visit Matira Beach
Don't vacation on the world's most celebrated island without walking along Bora Bora's longest stretch of pure, white sand. It's a public beach with

safe, shallow swimming, so everyone can enjoy time there. This is also a romantic vantage point for watching extraordinary sunsets.

The closed (and unlikely to re-open) Bora Bora Hotel on the north side of the beach was the first luxury hotel on the island. That's why its overwater bungalows mark the spot for fantastic snorkeling. They were built above some of the lagoon's largest coral heads, which are teeming with fish.

2. Shop in Vaitape

Bora Bora's main town, Vaitape, has a variety of stores to keep you entertained for a couple of hours. It's only a small village with tiny versions of the services you are accustomed to; banks, stores, a post office, a supermarket, and a church. The markets adjacent to the wharf are crammed with lovely handmade items that cost a few dollars.

3. Check out Bloody Mary's

Bloody Mary's has become an icon in Bora Bora. Its fame originates from the legendary musical, South Pacific, although the movie was actually filmed on another island. This restaurant/bar specializes in seafood but there's no need to buy a meal. For the cost of a drink you can hang out on a palm-trunk stool, under a thatched roof, with your feet on the sand.

You're likely to pass by Bloody Mary's on the way to or from Vaitape and Matira Beach. Stop in just to check out the exotic atmosphere, read the list of famous past visitors on the entrance wall, and see the surprising bathroom. A person of average fitness can easily walk from Matira beach to this popular oasis, so these two hot spots can be experienced together. *There's also a romantic jetty, for the rich and famous to arrive.*

4. Browse in Art Galleries

Looking is free. So visit the art galleries dotted around the Circle Island Road. They exhibit colorful works of talented, local artists. It's a way to see this exotic island through local eyes.

Galerie d'Art Pakalola is upstairs next to the post office in Vaitape, displaying paintings and other forms of art created by Polynesian artists. Phone (689) 70.75.60

Galerie d'Art Alain & Linda is on the beach side of Pofai Bay. It exhibits paintings, pottery, sculptures, lithographs and etchings, by the best-known Polynesian artists. They also stock pareos and tee shirts which Alain, a Frenchman, paints. Linda, a painter, originated from Germany but they have both lived in French Polynesia for over 30 years.
Phone (689) 67 70 32

Garrick Yrondi shows off his paintings, sculptures, bronzes, and collages in his Villa Rea Hana gallery which is located on the mountain side of the road behind the Boutique Gauguin in Amanahune.
Phone (689) 60 5715

Parara Mountain Artist exhibits Emmanuel Masson's paintings of Bora Bora and the Polynesian people. He was taught to paint by his father, Jean Masson, a well-known artist; who had four children with his favorite model and student, Rosine Temauri. This gallery is not on the Circle Island Road. If you want to find it yourself, turn off the main road, next to the church at Faanui, and follow the winding dirt road (marked with broken lines on tourist maps) until you spot the signage. There's a lovely view from the garden, which he allows visitors to picnic in, so stop at a market on the way to pick up lunch or a snack.
Phone (689) 67.65.31

Bora Bora Art Naea Studio on the mountain side of the Circle Island Road at Fanuii, also showcases the Polynesian art of Emmanuel Masson, as well as displaying a variety of gifts.
Phone: (689) 40 67 71 17

5. Cycle the Island Road

Like to be independent and active? Then create your own sightseeing adventure! You won't get lost on this island with one real road. Hire a bike and pedal around the 32 kilometers/20 miles of the Circle Island Road, stopping to see the scenic and historical attractions along the way. As its name indicates, this road runs right around the coastline, so you'll be rewarded by sensational views.

Pick up your wheels at one of the bike rental locations near Matira Beach.

Fit folk can ride the coastal road (which is quite flat and has only a couple of steep inclines) in 2 hours, without stops. The unfit can pay a little extra to hire an electric bike. How long you'll take depends on whether you go at a leisurely pace, stopping to see sights and take photographs, or whether you just want to just ride free as the wind.

During hot weather this open-air experience is more enjoyable first thing in the morning, or in the last hours of the day. When passing through Vaitape, remember to stop at Chin Lee's supermarket for the best selection of snacks and refreshments, at the very best prices.

Be Aware: *If you're planning to hire a bike, pack a bike-lock to secure it at stops.*

...or Tour with 4 Wheels and Buy Provisions
If you're staying in accommodation where you can provide some food of your own, consider hiring a car for a day to explore the circle island route, *and* stock up on provisions.

We caught a bus from our hotel to Vaitape, hired a car, and then stopped at Chin Lee's market to buy up big. Later, as we passed our hotel on the Circle Island Road, we dropped the supplies in the fridge of our room. Make sure you take carry bags from home as (out of respect for the lagoon and ocean) there's no plastic freely handed out.

As you head around the island you may see trees loaded with fruit. Much of this island is untamed, and tropical fruit grows wild for the picking. But if you see a tree absolutely dripping with fruit, assume that it's bitter to the taste, so has been ignored by the locals.

Hiring a car will cost about the same as paying for a bus tour which traverses the Circle Island Road, pointing out sights that are included in our resources chapter.

Head South on the Circle Island Road
It's best to head south from Vaitape as there's more of interest to see and do around the first half of this route. You may decide, for some reason, not to go the whole way around; so by heading south you'll experience the most interesting part of Bora Bora.

In the RESOURCES chapter, there's a detailed 'as you go' guide, outlining the main sights to watch out for as you pedal along. It includes places worth stopping, and what *not* to miss.

6. Free Use of a Glamorous Resort's Grounds

Most Bora Bora resorts welcome visitors to dine at their restaurants. Four Seasons is the only exception. But luxurious **St Regis,** on the same motu, allows guests from other hotels to lunch at its sparkling overwater restaurant, Lagoon. Renowned French chef, Jean Jacques, presides over hospitality at Lagoon.

For the cost of a dish you can eat overwater, in gleaming luxury, surrounded by extraordinary views across the lagoon to Bora Bora's main island. After lunch take a stroll around the extraordinary grounds and get a free taste of what a top hotel in Paradise offers. Wear your swimmers underneath and you can try out the pool, lagoonarium, or beach.

The secluded and romantic **Conrad Nui** is especially welcoming. Book for lunch or dinner and you can enjoy the afternoon relaxing around its infinity pool or lie lazily shaded, on a 2-person hammock, on the white sand beach. A casual all-day restaurant and bar is right on the beach with a sand floor. There's a small charge for Nui's shuttle boat service, which is paid at the floating reception before the return journey.

You don't have to sell your car and book the Four Seasons to have a great time in Bora Bora. If you stay in pension type accommodation, you still get to enjoy the awesome lagoon (which is what has made Bora Bora famous) for free. You're amongst the lucky few travelers who make it to this tropical paradise! But we suggest that, as you *have to eat,* having a meal at a gorgeous resort is a wonderful opportunity to savor a taste of some Bora Bora luxury. Just remember to dine small, and hang out big; so that you create an interesting outing for the lowest price.

This is where our No.1 tip for a Tahiti vacation comes in handy ... Always wear your swimmers! Don't miss a single opportunity to swim off a beautiful beach or in a glamorous pool.

7. Swim with Stingrays

Drop by the old Bora Bora Yacht Club for a drink; or one of the freshest fish lunches in Bora Bora, at a good price. Enjoy the bonus of swimming with friendly rays. You can also laze on the pontoon and watch the glowing orb of sun, slowly dropping and sinking into the ocean. For the cost of a cocktail, this is a great place to meet locals, as well as chat with fellow dreamers from all over the world.

8. Visit a Treasure Trove

While you're in the islands of Tahiti, find out what makes the lustrous lagoon gems, harvested in these waters, so unique and pricey. If the day is too hot, or too wet, or you just want a break from turquoise; you can head off to be entertained at a black pearl store. Ensure you can't weaken and splurge, rendering all of your other clever savings invalid. Leave your credit card safely in the security box in your room and phone Wendy at Arc en Ciel 87.71.98.89 for a complimentary pickup and a warm welcome. It's both fun *and* an informative experience.

Know How to Get Around

Traveling around will be different to any other vacation you've experienced. The airport is on its own island! And boat is a more common than taxis! So having a basic understanding of logistics in this water-world will save dollars, fun time, and frustration.

Getting from the Airport

Due to its unusual location, as part of the flight ticket, Air Tahiti offers passengers a **complimentary shuttle-boat trip between the airport motu and Vaitape**. You can save hundreds of dollars on transfers just by choosing accommodation on the mainland, or a motu resort, where it's possible to take advantage of this *free* lagoon ride.

On arrival **at Vaitape wharf you can hail a taxi** which will cost about $20, including luggage. Vaitape is the hub of Bora Bora so if there's not a car waiting, one will show up soon. Drivers know they can pick up passengers, when a ferry comes in.

If you stay in pension accommodation, it's likely that the owner will arrange to pick you up from Vaitape wharf. This is often a complimentary service, to encourage you to book.

Each resort set on a motu (tiny coral island) has its own shuttle-boat for transferring guests to and from the airport. All **resorts charge over $100 per person**, and this cost cannot be avoided when staying at some (otherwise) difficult to access motu resorts. Guests are greeted with fragrant leis by a momma (waiting at each resort's booth in the airport) picked up by boat, and escorted speedily across the lagoon for an even warmer Polynesian welcome at their chosen resort. You will remember that astonishing ride the rest of your life, so if you want this luxurious 'hello', accept the price and enjoy every second of VIP treatment.

But there are **three motu resorts which allow a very cheap and easy option**. If you stay at the **Sofitel Private Island** you can utilize the free boat-shuttle to Vaitape (provided by Air Tahiti) and then catch a taxi to the Sofitel Marara Beach Resort, on the main island. This taxi ride costs double the usual price, as a surcharge is added for bags. On arrival, you will be escorted to a little pier for free transfer across to the motu isle.

Similarly, if you book the **Intercontinental Thalasso** you can take the free airport shuttle to Vaitape and get a taxi to drop you at Intercontinental Le Moana. Intercontinental provides frequent, free, speedy shuttles between its motu resort and Le Moana, on the main island. The cost for either of these taxi trips will be about $20. So there's a huge saving while you still have comfortable transfers (which most tourist wouldn't know are possible). The **Pearl Beach** resort can also be accessed by taking the free shuttle to Vaitape and catching a taxi up the coast to the shuttle-boat base. From there you can ride the resort boat over to the motu.

Getting independently to the **Conrad Nui** is an even easier option, as their regular shuttle service, between the resort and the mainland, comes in to the Vaitape wharf. Just get off the airport boat and ask where to wait for the Conrad's shuttle to arrive. (It's only a small area.) You simply board the boat on the Vaitape side, as fees are only paid at Nui's reception when you intend visiting the main island.

Getting Around for Fun

By now you will realize that tariffs at motu resorts are higher than hotels on the mainland. Plus some motu resorts charge for their shuttle service between the resort and the mainland, and some courteously provide it for free.

The good news is that, to do some excursions, the tour provider will pick you up right from your resort's dock on the motu (at no extra charge). For others you will be asked to take the resort's shuttle-boat across to where it docks on the mainland and be picked up from there.

Before you decide on a hotel, find out what the bottom line will be, so there are no surprises along the way, to spoil careful budgeting. But don't only think about how to *save* money. Also, pay attention to *milking the most value* from what you do decide to spend!

Some folk just want to secret themselves away on a motu resort and relax. Are you planning to spend most of your time recharging on a sun lounge, cooling down in the sensational lagoon, and occasionally go for a row? Or are you the type/s who want to dash about? Two gorgeous resorts, the *Intercontinental Thalasso and the Sofitel Private Island, offer the best of both* scenarios. They're situated out on motus while also offering regular complimentary shuttle boats to the main island.

All motu resorts run a few daily buses between their dock on the mainland, and the main town of Vaitape. This allows guests to visit Matira Beach or Vaitape for an outing. Depending on the resort policy, the service may incur an extra charge.

Questions to Ask Before Booking a Resort

- What time does the boat shuttle service start in the morning, and end in the evening?
- How frequently does the shuttle boat go to and fro?
- What happens if you miss the last boat? (Water taxis are few and pricey!)
- Are there charges to use it? Does it cost more in the evening?
- What times does a bus go to Vaitape, via Matira; and return to the resort's dock?
- Is there another charge for the bus trip?
- What free beach and cultural activities does each resort offer, outdoors and in?
- What in-house wet weather activities does the resort provide if it rains?

Know the Taxi Charges

There's not a single traffic light, stop sign, or even actual crossroads on

Bora Bora's main island road. So it's easy to gauge the fare between destinations. Before you get into a taxi ask how much the trip will cost. You'll probably need to (have reception) phone for a taxi, unless you're waiting in Vaitape, where they show up regularly. This is not Sydney, or New York! You rarely see taxis cruising for passengers. It's such an out of the way, small island, with few possible clients during the larger part of the year. The fare may be set a little higher than for the same distance back home, but because traffic always flows smoothly, the price evens out.

We had one experience where the driver asked for double the usual charge. We knew it was incorrect because previously we had paid the equivalent of less than $10 to go between the Sofitel and Vaitape. When we told him it was too much, he pulled out a sheet and showed us the figure. But we recognized that he was flashing a plasticized sheet of the charges that included luggage, so we took a more honest taxi.

Keep in mind that *after 7 pm taxi charges increase* and they're hard to find. Don't be caught on Matira Beach after sunset, without arrangements to get back to your hotel in place...unless you have a phone or Olympic legs! One evening we had to walk back to Bloody Mary's and then saved on a taxi, because before we could find one, a handsome young Frenchman (with three words of English) gave us a ride. It felt safe and was a fun way to save.

That worked out so well that we held our thumbs out (when necessary) on another vacation. It was New Year's Day, and most of the islanders were out on private motus celebrating. There wasn't a hire-car or taxi available. *We* didn't have hangovers and wanted to explore. While walking around the Circle Island Road we became tired and hot, so accepted a ride from a local Polynesian couple. They asked if we'd like to drive around the entire island! It wasn't just a scenic ride. We were treated to an infant teacher (with perfect English) sharing more tidbits of daily island life and history than we've ever heard from tour guides. On the way, we stopped to see her classroom (directly under the shadow of Mt Otemanu) where the children's handmade Polynesian Christmas decorations were still hanging up. We saved big on the best Bora Bora tour ever!

Hire a Bike

Little Bora Bora is perfect for cycling. The Circle Island Road is mostly flat and runs around the perimeter (with just a couple of steep inclines) so captures continuous views across the lagoon. This is one of the few holiday destinations where we save money, by not having to hire a car, and actually see more by bike. There are very few vehicles on the road (mostly scooters) and no cross streets to negotiate, so it's an extremely safe ride.

But don't think that you can go exploring the interior by bike. Even a hire car can't go there. The dirt roads were made by U.S soldiers to set up lookouts, and coastal guns, during world war 11. Tracks have not been maintained and are strewn with ruts from erosion. It takes a decent level of fitness, or a 4x4 safari jeep, to navigate the rugged inland, and can only done on an organized excursion, or by hiking.

Forget Public Transport

Some Tahitian islands have good public transport in the form of le truck. On Bora Bora le truck is now a bus which runs in conjunction with school and ferry times. But it can be unreliable, so don't waste valuable vacation time (which is money) waiting around for it.

Free Transport!

Book a meal at any of the best Bora Bora restaurants and they will provide you with free transport each way. We once had lunch at the St Regis Resort and spent the afternoon in its beautiful grounds. Towards evening, we asked the concierge to book our dinner at the Kaina Hut, and took the free St Regis shuttle boat back to the main island dock. A free taxi was already waiting for us as we left the boat. After eating, the taxi took us to the Vaitape wharf where we caught the boat back to our villa at the Nui (which has a later shuttle than most motu resorts). Combining these two experiences meant smooth transitions, without spending a franc to return.

Must Knows!

Free Internet

Using the internet at Bora Bora hotels can be costly, even for a short time. If you are really counting dollars, Boutique Fareaui across the road from Le Moana at Matira Beach gives free internet access (you can use their computer) when you make a purchase. This impressively stocked store has a wide range of goods and souvenirs, including fair priced water.

Beware of Room Phone Charges!

Don't get caught with a huge phone bill when you check out. In other words, don't pick up the phone in your room unless it's to call housekeeping! The rates sting because calling between motus is a long-distance call, and there is no competition between telecommunication companies out in the blue yonder. I learnt this hard fact at my resort's front desk after I was handed a bill with $370 for telephone use. I did not *phone home*! The charges were incurred at a motu resort, from just two calls to chat with tour providers on the main island. After I stood my ground, complaining sweetly, the manager on duty cut the figure in half, probably to get me out of earshot of other guests. I still wasn't impressed by the charges.

Complain Nicely

Often, it's not *what* you say that matters, but *how* you say it. Remember why you came on this vacation. If necessary, take time out to calm yourself before you react. Usually the person you're addressing wasn't even the cause of the problem. Treat her with the respect that you are asking for yourself. Keep in mind that you are not the only guest on the island who wants the vacation of a lifetime. Demanding or insisting is more likely have the opposite effect to what you intend. You may be surprised by what goodness comes your way if you are nice.

Switch into Island Time

Travel reviews are mostly done by folk sharing their amazing Bora Bora adventures. But sometimes you'll read opinions from irate travelers, complaining that the service wasn't snappy enough for their (usually American) standards. We know (and love) how amazing service in the U.S. is, but highly recommend that when you sit on the Air Tahiti plane you relax your benchmarks, and your frantic frontal lobe, and everything will turn out frangipani!

Many of the Polynesian workers who do the mundane, physical work possess a different sense of time to westerners. They're gentle, friendly, humble (yet proud) folk. If you've sent for fresh towels and they haven't arrived in 2 minutes, don't get into a flap thinking that *you* (and *only* you) aren't important. Don't take it personally! Just switch into "island time" and you'll receive the most value and fun for your vacation investment.

Free Evenings

Out here every evening feels relaxing; in a fully alive kind of way. Look up at **the starry, starry, night!** There's no need to spend money on entertainment. It's free. The nearest city is half a world away so the night skies are incredibly, unbelievably clear. You'll spot constellations like the Southern Cross and the Big Dipper; and the only sound you'll hear is the soft lap, lap of the lagoon.

Linger over dinner, walk on the beach, stroll around the gardens, or hang out listening to music in the resort bar. On one evening go to a vantage point for watching the sun's orb sink gradually into the ocean. Feel the serenity.

Bora Bora has only **one night club, Le Recif** (The Reef), located north of Vaitape, on the way to Faanui. We haven't tried it but you don't have to spend much on an entry fee to check out the distinctly Polynesian atmosphere in the dark, crowded room. We've heard that the dancing and drinking goes well into the wee hours of morning.

You Don't Need a Dictionary

Although French and Tahitian are the official languages in French Polynesia**, English is understood by most** staff at resorts, and many other folk in major tourist areas. There's no need to walk around with a dictionary in your hand.

In the words of Jan Prince, one of the most widely traveled writers about Tahiti, "...you can get by with English, gestures and smiles almost everywhere you go in these islands."

Learn to Read a French Menu

For some of you this is the time to brush up on your old-school French. You'll be so pleased with yourself if you can figure out what's in the dishes offered on the fancy French menus, or get want you want at the supermarket! On my first visit, *my* school French was so rusty that at Carrefour we had to cluck, and then quack, with arms flapping; to find out if the pate was chicken or duck.

Save Saying "I Do"

Couples can honeymoon at Bora Bora resorts, like celebrities, for a discounted price. That official piece of paper saying 'just married' gives you many privileges in Bora Bora, where resorts favor honeymooners. You also have a good chance of being up-graded, especially if you avoid peak season. Enjoying your honeymoon in Tahiti will be the best value Tahiti vacation you can have in your life.

Bora Bora resorts excel at creating romantic experiences and interludes that infuse magic into a honeymoon. They have a bottle of French champagne on ice in your room at arrival, and there may be pareos and a Tahitian pearl laid out. Each day a little gift, such as a piece of shell jewelry, is placed on the bed. Some of the Bora Bora resorts provide a complimentary couples pampering in their exotic spa, and a dinner on the beach; as treats for each honeymoon couple. For example, St Regis, (where the butler service can organize almost anything) serves a romantic, free dinner on the beach overlooking the lagoon.

Set Up a Wedding Gift Registry

If you're planning to honeymoon in Bora Bora, choose a resort which offers a wedding gift registry. Most do. Heading the pack (for attention to detail) is the very private St Regis, which now has a whole department for creating wonderful weddings. Other resorts are doing things very nicely too. The best priced chapel wedding would be at Le Meridian and the staff there take great pride in organizing special occasions.

Invite family and friends to help make your dream of an affordable tropical island honeymoon come true. It will make gift giving easy for them.

Choose an All-inclusive Honeymoon Package

One way to get a better price on the whole vacation is to select from the many available 'ready-to-go' honeymoon packages that have extras thrown in.

Or you can create your own custom designed honeymoon by collaborating with a specialist Tahiti travel agent. To ensure a seamless Bora Bora vacation for the best price choose an expert who also offers support *during* your honeymoon vacation. Check out the one we have listed in our resources section, at the end. Most likely your whole trip will cost less and you have the assurance that every detail will be taken care of, even if a glitch occurs while you're away.

Marry on the Beach...

Unless you have your heart set upon marrying in a wedding chapel, you can save big by leaving out the expense of having a ceremony in your resort's private chapel. A romantic, and meaningful, alternative is to exchange vows in a service on the beach, officiated over by a marriage celebrant. This can be as simple or as elaborate as you choose, depending on your taste and budget. All you need to pay for is a celebrant, and as many islanders playing instruments (and dancing) as you wish.

Be aware: *If you 'tie the knot' in the grounds of your resort, you must use their personnel, which includes everyone from hairdresser to photographer to celebrant.*

In Moorea?
Thinking outside the square gives another excellent option that will enable you to trim hundreds, or thousands off your vacation, depending on your choices. By now you will probably realize that the price of Bora Bora accommodation is the highest in Tahiti. A cheaper and more flexible option again is to *marry in Moorea and then fly on to Bora Bora for your honeymoon.*

Or Bora Bora?
We understand that you may have been dreaming of a Bora Bora wedding and that's what you want. So here's a way to make it memorable, while cutting down on expenses. It's possible to book a celebrant who's also an

expert on Tahiti vacations. Have her arrange your wedding in Bora Bora, on a perfect white-sand private motu, and enjoy your remaining honeymoon days staying on another gorgeous island, which offers a high standard of accommodation, while costing much less.

Bespoke Weddings in Bora Bora

If couples arrange services themselves, Bora Bora weddings can be individually personalized, *and* have smaller price tag. This enables you to design something different, and hire only the individual providers of your choice. To_create your own signature wedding, on a private motu in Bora Bora you will need to connect with a licensed Tahiti wedding planner and marriage celebrant. Our Tahiti vacation specialist can also organize this for you.

Proposing in Bora Bora ?

Congratulations on your choices of; commitment, and island. There is no lovelier venu on earth to go down on your knees and ask the love of our life to be in your life; forever after. No one could say no on this entrancing island. You don't have to spend a cent to set the scene. Ukuleles are playing, intoxicating perfume wafts through the air, and a visual feast surrounds you. Return to the front cover of this book for the photo of the tiny isle with one hammock. It's our top suggestion for where to go. Where will you find it? In shallow lagoon water just off the InterContinental's beach.

Make a Special Request

If you want to make a special occasion *even* more special, without spending more, you can email the hotel's general manager and ask for an upgrade. Either call the hotel reception directly, or first google to find the name of your hotel's general manager. Hotels regularly get requests for free upgrades so *don't expect* one. But it is possible. Just appreciate the special treatment if it happens. They're given more frequently in 4 or 5 star hotels than in cheaper ones. General managers love you to have a wonderful experience at their hotel and sometimes go out of the way to make guests feel welcome.

For help in writing your request, see the RESOURCES section. Luckily you won't have to write in French!

Resources

Where to Stay...in a Nutshell!

This is for the super-busy, the dyslexic, the lazy, or the confused; who are *dreaming* of a vacation on the world's most beautiful island; and *wrestling* with how to best make their money go around. Much of a Bora Bora vacation revolves around where you choose to stay:

To stay at a prestigious resort while knowing you're getting most value for $$ spent:
St Regis Beachfront or Overwater bungalow in the shoulder season. Book through a Tahiti specialist travel agent to get a bargain bundle.

To spend the least you can, and have an ultimate Bora Bora luxury experience:
Intercontinental Thalasso overwater bungalow; Conrad Nui Hillside or Garden bungalow; or Le Meridien overwater bungalow. Plan to go off peak and book through a dedicated Tahiti travel agent, to get special prices, plus extras thrown in.

To stay at a lovely Polynesian style resort, offering island ambiance; without spending more than you need:
Pearl Beach beach bungalow, Intercontinental Le Moana overwater bungalow or Sofitel Private Island bungalows.

To have a true Bora Bora experience, with the smallest price tag:
Sofitel Marara Beach Garden Bungalow, Conrad Nui Lagoon View suite, Intercontinental Le Moana beach bungalow.

To know you're in Bora Bora 24/7, even with a teensy budget:
Maitai Ocean View rooms

Don't mind roughing it to see the best parts of the world?
Pick from the pensions with direct access to Matira Beach.

Choose the above option that fits your situation, add in a circle island boat tour, use our insider information on how to eat and drink for less in Bora Bora, and *you don't need to spend on anything more* to have a sparkling vacation with cherished memories.

You may want to check out what the cost will be to book yourself, and if you stumble upon an awesome deal, it's very exciting. Remember that if you choose a 4 or 5 star resort, you'll usually find that if you ask the experts at Pacific For Less *to do the work* for you, the prices and service are as good as it gets!

Writing a Room Request

Express excitement about your upcoming stay, but also be short and to the point when asking. Managers are busy people so don't like verbose emails. Include your reservation confirmation numbers and your hotel elite status. If there's a specific room or view you want, mention it. Indicate that you know that he/she may not be able to do it, but you would appreciate your request being honored if the hotel does have vacancy.

Just happen to slip in that you are excited about trying their famous restaurant, or indulging in their tropical spa; and you may have more chance. General managers like you creating revenue for their hotel.
Don't demand special treatment. Remember that it's easy to say *no* to rude people ... or ignore them! It's more difficult to deny a sweet honeymoon couple; or a guest who's eagerly looking forward to visiting your hotel, to celebrate a milestone event.

Don't expect to get automatically upgraded if you have used points to purchase your room. In that case you might be asked to contribute some cash. But it may happen, especially if you have *elite* status with the chain. There's nothing to lose by asking.

An Example of a Request Letter:

"Dear Mr Ben Evolent,
My girlfriend, Mandy, and I have booked to stay at your wonderful hotel

108

and are looking forward to experiencing the Hilltop Spa that we have heard so much about. Our party has reserved two beach villas for October the 7th to the 14th. We are very excited about our long-awaited vacation and, what Mandy doesn't know, is that I am intending to propose while on Bora Bora.

Is it possible for you to upgrade us to an overwater bungalow? And, vacancy permitting, can our friends, John and Sue Smith have a villa nearby? I know that you may not be in a position to do this, but will greatly appreciate if you can organize this extra surprise for my beautiful lady.
Thank you,
Don Juan

Our Top Picks of Islands

French Polynesia has over 100 islands. Deciding *which ones* to visit is a journey in itself. To make it easy we're suggesting the best islands to see with ease, in conjunction with Bora Bora, and telling what's fun about each:

The Scenic, Adventure Island

The island of **Moorea is a superb add-in to the beginning or end of a Bora Bora vacation**. Moorea is an easy 30 minute ferry ride from the main island of Tahiti, where international flights arrive. This saves the cost of another flight fare, plus the extra time allocation that's necessary for showing up at an airport before departure. You only need to be at the dock, in downtown Papeete, 20 minutes before the boat leaves.

Moorea is so sensationally scenic that it's the favorite vacation spot of French Polynesians themselves! Many come yearly; from isolated, outer islands; and get together here with friends and family. We too have enjoyed wonderful stays on Moorea. It's such a complimentary island to add to a Bora Bora vacation.

I love the smug way Mooreans smile while saying that "Bora Bora may have the most beautiful lagoon, but Moorea has the most beautiful island!"

There's a vast, lush, inner island with spectacular scenery to explore; and engaging activities to get around and do. In contrast, much of your time in Bora Bora, will be spent relaxing around the turquoise lagoon, admiring the verdant, volcanic isle as an awesome scenic backdrop.

Moorea is a wonderful *secret pick for an affordable wedding in Tahiti*. The Tahiti wedding celebrant recommended by our reliable travel agent lives there. Guests can have great accommodation here, without paying the prices of Bora Bora. After the celebrations, the bride and groom can fly onwards to Bora Bora for a dream honeymoon.

Moorea boasts many *more budget-friendly options* than Bora Bora, and they're all in incredible locations. There are several lovely resorts providing overwater bungalows for a fraction of the price of Bora Bora.

Our pick of resorts on Moorea is the Hilton. In fact, in all of Tahiti it may be our favorite place to stay! Every perfect inch of the resort is gorgeous, and the surrounding panorama is *breathtaking*. You'll save big by booking your overwater stay here and you can jump straight from your deck for fantastic snorkeling. The beach and garden villas are lovely too. Each has its own very private plunge-pool, even though you're only a few steps from a pristine white-sand beach.

While many resorts *claim* to have coral gardens with snorkeling opportunities, the Moorea Hilton actually *has abundant living, coral right off its expansive beach* and under the overwater bungalows. Even beginners can comfortably wade in and safely enjoy the delights of snorkeling amongst a multitude of curious, colorful fish. We think this Hilton gives superb value for money.

If you want **to spend even less on accommodation**, Moorea offers a wide choice of pensions and vacation rentals that sell for a fraction of the cost of staying at a resort, and some are close to the water. **Hotel Les Tipaniers**, located on a beautiful beach, is a good alternative if you want a small-priced hotel stay.

Bora Bora as the Backdrop!

Want to see Bora Bora even when you aren't on Bora Bora? A stay at the lovely **Le Taha'a Resort** will provide you with Bora Bora's majestic peak, Mt Otemanu, as the backdrop. Little-known Le Taha'a island has only one resort and it can have attractive specials offering up to 50% off. If Taha'a appeals to you, look out for one of these deals and jump on it immediately. Most of this island remains as untouched jungle and there's a variety of interesting things to see.

Le Taha'a Boasts Three Bests:

1. Best drift snorkel in Tahiti

Not far from the resort there's a narrow channel of coral gardens offering one of the best snorkeling adventures in all of Tahiti. Catch the tide at the right time of day and the slow-moving current provides a sublime drift snorkeling experience, viewing a diversity of neon fish amongst brightly colored coral.

This experience is so perfect it could have been created by Disney. The water's not deep, but you do need to be grown up enough to negotiate your body parts slowly through a passageway, lined with coral which is home to curious, tropical fish.

Be aware: *Make sure that you can float and dog paddle, and you've enough prior experience to feel comfortable in the water with your snorkeling gear on.*

2. Best prices on black pearls

Taha'a is home to small family pearl farms and a visit, that's both entertaining and educational, can be arranged. It's an opportunity to purchase exquisite Tahitian pearls, in lustrous pastel hues, at a discounted price compared to what you would pay in a boutique on Bora Bora, or in Papeete.

On a trip to Ferme Perliere Champon we watched a demonstration of the spherical, aragonite nucleus being inserted into oysters as a perfect base for the mother-of-pearl coating. Afterwards, the lady of the house, Monique, made us comfortable in a lovely room in her home, and spoke about the different types of pearls. What a pleasure it was to sit surrounded by a fairy-tale assortment of pastel colored pearls, with the fragrance of flowering tropical foliage drifting in the pretty French windows. There's no need to shop till you drop trying to find gorgeous pearls for the best price.

3. World's best flavored vanilla

Did you know that the superior taste of Tahitian vanilla is prized by top chefs around the world? Taha'a, alias the *vanilla* isle, has one of the few farms still cultivating by the natural method of training the vanilla vines to grow up existing vegetation. You can visit for free and gain insights into the growing and processing of this popular spice.

We were dropped by boat at La Vallee de la Vanille and had a superb experience. I used this rare opportunity to buy the highest quality plump vanilla pods (that we never see back home) for a very favorable price. I just break off an inch and add it to other ingredients in my high-speed blender, for an OMG smoothie. To make my own superior tasting vanilla essence I soak beans in vodka.

Want to Skip Resort Prices?

Taha'a also has several types of cheaper pension style accommodation in the form of little huts set in pretty gardens, all near water, and some offer views across the ocean to Bora Bora. To save even more money by having a simpler stay, check out L'Hibiscus, which also houses a restaurant and yacht club; Au phil du temps; and Pension Titaina.

Getting to Le Taha'a is Glorious

To travel to Le Taha'a from Bora Bora you fly above awesome views and land on the more populated neighbouring island, Raiatea. (With what a helicopter tour over these spectacular waters costs per minute, consider it a cut-price excursion!) The resort's private shuttle-boat will pick you up from there and treat you to an entrancing 35-minute ride of beautiful coastal navigation, with Taha'a on one side, and the silhouette of Bora Bora on the other.

Or, if you have saved heaps on your accommodation with the 50% off deal, you might want to use the savings on a helicopter flight straight from Bora Bora to Tahaa. *Wink, wink!*

The Garden Isle

Huahine is a quiet, pristine island with only a few places to stay. As demand for this island is lower, there are far less tourists, and accommodation prices are cheaper. Don't let the lower tourist numbers fool you though. Huahine, affectionately called the garden isle, is remarkably beautiful. It's only less visited as it is less known! Shhh, don't tell too many people about it!

There are three 'hotels' on Huahine, all priced around $200 per night. We can recommend **Relais Mahana**. It's located on a lovely beach, with proximity to Fare, the main town on Huahine. To get to Huahine from Bora Bora you will need to fly, so take the airfare price into consideration. Better still, take advantage of the cost saving Bora pass listed in the inter-flight section.

Far Out in the Blue Yonder

You can enjoy budget priced accommodation in one of the most unique and unspoiled places on earth. Go out to the **Tuamotu Atolls** and stay at a friendly local pension. Few tourists venture way out there so you'll be treated like royalty.

We can highly recommend **Pension Paparara** which is also a dive-lodge located right at the water's edge. Many other wanderers agree with our recommendation, as Paparara won the Tripadvisor Certificat d'Excellence in 2014. Out in these pristine waters, divers can have the thrill of plunging into some of the world's most stunning underwater scenery.

If this is part of your dream, you can really save on the airfare to fly out here. *Check back in the inter-island flights section.* For those who want to visit the atolls and are time-rich; there is now a fantastic new freighter, the

Aranui V, which sleeps passengers at various levels of comfort. This boat departs from Papeete and travels beyond the Tuamotus, as it serves as a lifeline for 6 islands in the remote Marquesas. It also stops at Rangiroa. There's a level of pricing for everyone.

Contact Details

Tahiti Specialist Travel Agent

Pacific For Less

Claudia and Jennifer, at Pacific For Less, specialize exclusively in booking French Polynesian vacations. Based on Maui in Hawaii, they have grateful clients all over the world. They're familiar with what Bora Bora offers, from their own family holiday experience. Their chosen niche involves liaising (smooching up to) and negotiating with the 4 and 5 star resorts, plus tour providers; to offer near wholesale prices, with extras thrown in.

Like us, they're dedicated to making Bora Bora vacations the best they can be. *Their* chosen focus is satisfying those seeking *luxury*. Such people have high standards; yet we've not heard a single complaint about Claudia and Jennifer, only praise. You'll receive a full personalized service, without the high-end, travel-company prices! They're conveniently located in the same time zone as Tahiti; and clients are given Claudia's personal cell phone number to call if any issues arise or something is not meeting expectations.

Boat Hire

La Plage

Boat hire is available between 8.30am and 5.30pm. Telephone: 28-48-66
Before showing up for your boat hire, we suggest you visit the minimart
that's just a few meters south down the road from la Plage. Get yourself
drinks and any other provisions that will help make your day out.

Tahitian Terms

Tahiti and Her Isles - This romantic (and sometimes confusing) term was
inspired by a Tahiti Tourist office campaign for promoting relaxing
vacations to busy executives; and the affectionate phrase stuck. It refers
to the most populated group of islands, the Society Islands; which are
located furthest west in French Polynesia. The Societies are divided into
the Windward Islands, which includes Tahiti, the largest therefore the main
island (where you arrive); and the Leeward Islands where Bora Bora lies.

Atoll - a low lying coral island
Barrier reef - coral reef that divides the lagoon from the ocean
Coral - white calcareous structure inhabited by organisms which make up
colorful, living polyps inside skeletal pores
Lagoon - (usually) calm body of water inside a coral reef
Motu - small coral island inside the lagoon
Leeward - the downwind side, sheltered from prevailing winds
Nacre - mother of pearl coating produced by an oyster
Keshi - miss-shaped pearl which had nucleus rejected
Baguette - French long, crusty, bread stick
Gendarmerie - French police station
Magasin - food store
Plat du jour - special of the day

Sing a Few Polynesian Words

Learning a little local lingo always adds to our holiday spirit; and builds rapport. Don't be shy about trying a few (unusual sounding) words. You'll add a cultural dimension to your vacation experience and also receive more personal attention from the islanders you meet. For a very long time, the only language allowed to be spoken, at school or work, was French. But now times have changed and Tahitian is actually taught in schools.

Surprisingly, there are only 13 letters in the traditional, local alphabet, so there's a lot of repetition, especially of vowels, which can seem confusing at first. Let go of the rhythms of spoken English and adopt the sing song voice and bouncy intonations of the Tahitians.

Notice that there is no 'B'. In fact, the Tahitian alphabet has no hard consonants at all. If you are curious about how you can be planning a trip to 'Bora Bora', it's because the first Europeans to arrive mistakenly heard 'P' as 'B'. Thereafter Bora Bora became the accepted name for Pora Pora. On my first vacation a mischievous guide told me (with a serious face) that the first arrivals named their discovery 'Bora' meaning, beautiful. They repeated 'Bora' to adequately describe the island. Looking around from the tour boat I naively believed him.

A ... pronounced 'ar' as in farm

E ... a short 'e' sound'

F ... sounds like 'fa' in far

H ... sounds like 'he' in hen

I ... sounds like 'ee' in deep

M ... pronounced 'mo' as in most

N ... sounds like 'nu' as in noon

O ... pronounced like 'o' as in so

P ... 'p'

R ... pronounced like 'ro' in rope

T ... 't'

U ... pronounced oo like in soon

V ... 'v'

Say thank you "mauruuru" in Polynesian and watch faces light up. Ask the Polynesians you meet how to say (and pronounce) basic expressions and they'll be pleased to fill you in.

Bora Bora Villages

Most of Bora Bora's 7,000 inhabitants live in three villages, at the edge of the lagoon.

Vaitape, the main village has most of the shops, several banks, a post office, and a church. This is the town of interest to travelers.

Anau can be seen from the lagoon and resorts around the eastern motu rings. Just look for the church spire which acts as the landmark.

Faanui is at the head of the bite shaped bay on Bora Bora's north-west side and is also recognizable by the church steeple piercing the skyline. Other inhabitants live out on small motus in the lagoon. To get to school or work they go by boat to the mainland, and then catch a bus, or are picked up by a relative.

Bora Bora's Grand Cultural Month

Every July, the Heiva Festival, (which was first staged in Bora Bora) is held on each of the Tahiti's most populated islands. It's a grand excuse to get competitive while showcasing Polynesian dance and culture. It turns traditional arts and skills into entertaining sporting events. But don't think for a moment it's all for tourism ... the islanders have the most fun. Don't fret if you're not visiting in July. It's the most expensive time of year. And most hotels offer Polynesian dance shows at least once a week, all year round. Occasionally they include some awesome fire dancing and that's more likely on Tahiti, the main island. When talking to a travel consultant, check if you can see some fire dancing during your vacation dates.

Which Local Dish is a "Must"?

Don't leave Tahiti without trying this addictive national dish. Made from raw tuna or mahi-mahi, marinated in lime juice and coconut milk, it's usually the freshest choice on a menu and offers good food value for money.

What Time is it in Bora Bora?

All of "Tahiti and Her Isles" is located in the same time zone as Hawaii, which is three hours behind Los Angeles and six hours behind New York. This changes when the United States moves to Daylight Savings Time. Between November and March the difference changes to two hours behind on the west coast, and five hours behind on the east coast. Synchronize your watch with local time by turning it (the above number of hours ahead) when you land in Papeete.

Find the Facts in Fiction

Both the Pearl Beach and Marara Beach resorts have a showing of 'Mutiny on the Bounty". Some scenes, in both the 1962 Marlon Brando version and the later 1984 Mel Gibson retelling, were shot on Tahiti, Moorea and Bora Bora. They perpetuate the legend that the infatuated sailors on the *HMS Bounty* revolted because they didn't want to leave the hospitality of the sensual local women behind.

The Polynesian bungalows that are now part of the Sofitel Marara Beach Resort, on the main island of Bora Bora, were especially built to house the actors and crew while making the 1962 movie.

Bora Bora's Circle Island Road Tour

Heading south from Vaitape boat dock you'll be traveling along the water's edge. Keep your peripheral vision open, so that you also notice the many opportunities for **spectacular glimpses of Mt Otemanu**, towering above on the left.

At the edge of town you'll spot two pearl boutiques, **La Perla** and **Robert Wan's**. Next on the bayside you'll spy **Moon Bed and Breakfast** which offers low budget accommodation.

Soon you'll see **Alain and Linda's art gallery** which is usually announced by a clothesline laden with bright pareos waving in the breeze. It's worth stopping to peruse the artworks.

Shortly you'll be passing **Olympia, a big sporting complex**, instantly recognizable by the oval outside. Rugby, soccer, and volleyball matches are held here. On Wednesday and Friday afternoons the competitive atmosphere is transformed by the rhythm of dance classes being held for children, teens and adults. Every Saturday a canoe race, paga paga, sets out from here and ends at Matira Beach. The skate park, located in this complex also holds regular bicycle races.

On the opposite side of the road to the big sporting grounds, there's a **track winding across the island to the small village of Anau**, on the east coast. You'll pass through Anau later on. There are only a few tracks in Bora Bora's rugged inland because when the missionaries arrived they insisted that the islanders move down from the high, jungle interior, where they had felt safe dwelling, and live along the flat perimeter. This enabled the patriarchal church to control their daily lives and practices. The few dirt roads that exist were forged by the U.S. navy during WWII and are now rutted and in disrepair. They can only be used by foot or mountain bike, and some can be negotiated by a dedicated 4x4 safari jeep.

Continuing along the Circle Island Road you'll pass the well-known **Kaina Hut Restaurant** (French chef, Polynesian style recipes), much-lauded **Villa Mahana** (French chef, delicious and pricey French style cuisine integrating island flavors and ingredients), and notorious **Bloody Mary's**. We suggest you take a break here. Refresh by checking out the interesting bathroom. Then sip a delicious Tahiti cocktail while relaxing on a trunk stool, with your feet in the sand. But don't bother with the food!

The above 3 restaurants are all on the left side, or as they say in Bora Bora, the "mountain side" of the road. On the right side, the "lagoon side", you'll spot **The Farm of Bora Bora Pearl Company**. But give it a miss if you find lucky dips tempting. You might end up paying far too much for opening an oyster to reveal...a lack-lustre pearl...which is yours to keep. From here, if you look right across the bay to the left end of **Motu Toopua Iti,** you can see the few **Nui Resort's overwater bungalows** that offer views through to Mt Otemanu.

"Iti" is the Polynesian word for "warrior" and the Toopua motu has sacred boulders (up near the Hilltop Spa) which form part of legends about Hero, including his dog's paw.

Further south, at **Raititi Point** you'll notice the entrance to the (now closed) **Hotel Bora Bora**, which was the first luxury hotel on the island.

Much to the disappointment of devoted fans, who loved to holiday at Hotel Bora Bora, it's been closed for years, with no likelihood of re-opening. To make the proposed extensive improvements to keep this resort financially viable, the owners were given responsibility for the expense of relocating the Circle Island Road further in, so that it wouldn't go through the middle of the resort when more buildings were added. That brought plans to a halt.

Once you pass the **Bora Diving Center** and the **Bora Bora Gallery**, keep an eye out (on the mountain side) for a little track leading to a battery of huge coastal guns that are **remaining relics of WWII.** Several of these defence stations were set up by U.S. forces but the soldiers were never in action. (Unless you count the many blue-eyed babies that were left when they went back home). You can visit the cannons by hiking for 10 minutes up the trail on the east of the (now closed) Matira restaurant. The view will be worth the effort, and you'll save around $100 each, by doing it yourself, instead of taking a rough 4x4 safari jeep tour, which drives you to the guns as they were placed at great viewing points.

When you continue circling the main island, you'll see a well-signed **Ben's Place** (on the mountain side of the road) offering typical American comfort food. Ben the cook is an islander married to Robin, a friendly American woman who's been there long enough to be almost as brown as her hubby. On the days when a ship comes in, she represents tour companies on the wharf, advising re excursions, so if you've got any questions about the island, she'll have answers in perfect English.

Continuing on the route, you'll spot the old tree trunk holding up the roof of **Snack Matira**, which serves simple Polynesian style food and refreshments, all day, and into the evening.

Follow the **Point Matira** sign, indicating a turn-off to the right. This will bring you to the central area of fabulous, 2-mile-long, Matira beach, voted one of the world's best beaches. It's the only *public* beach on the main island of Bora Bora and will be a highlight of your day's tour.
Our golden rule in Bora Bora is to always wear swimmers. Heed the advice and have them ready under your clothers

The **Intercontinental Le Moana Resort** and **Hotel Matira** are both situated next to this magnificent stretch of white sand. Take a stroll around

Le Moana"s gorgeous flowering gardens, and Polynesian style communal areas, which integrate the talents of traditional artisans. The bar and restaurants offer wonderful views, and the food is good, so this would be a perfect lunch stop if your budget allows it, and you time it right. The salmon dish is our favorite, but you can have delicious burgers and simpler fare for less.

If you want a tasty meal for less, we can highly recommend **Snack Matira** which is across the road from the entrance to Le Moana. If you only want drinks, for the best price, buy them at **Boutique Fareaui** which is directly across the road from Le Moana's entrance.

When you continue on the Circle Island Road, you'll see another lunch (breakfast, or dinner) choice on the right side, **Fareau Manui**. This delightful restaurant has all-day eating. There are pages of menu offering about 30 choices of oven fried pizza, a huge assortment of burgers and paninis, plus French gastronomic dishes in the evening.

Fareau Manui also serves as a watering hole for Hotel Matira guests, and **Village Temanuata**, which you will notice several doors further along, fronting the beach. This quaint little family hotel offers some of the cheapest priced, individual Polynesian huts, on the island.

From here the road heads north up the east coast and a few minutes further on you'll pass by **Le Maitai**. Unless you're aware and alert you won't realize that you are actually passing *through* the hotel. The beach and overwater bungalows are on the right side, along with a restaurant, and the bulk of the hotel is on the left, with accommodation extending up the hillside.

As you pedal on, watch out for **La Bounty Restaurant, Tiare Market**, and **Nemo World** dive shop, all on the mountain side. Tiare looks small from the outside but you will be amazed at the variety of delicacies that are stacked up on the shelves. It's a worthwhile stop, which you may want to return to, if you're staying on this side of Bora Bora.

Proceeding further, the **Sofitel Marara Beach** will come into sight on the lagoon side. From here you'll have the closest view across the lagoon to the Sofitel Private Island, which you will have been noticing, just a short distance out, since arriving at Matira Point.

Next there's a steep incline that takes you up over the brilliant hues of **Faaopore Bay**, and past the closed, Club Med resort, that has now been acquired by an Australian businessman. Just before **Paoaoa Point** you can take a tunnel under the road (or walk up steps just past the boutique), to get up onto the ridge and visit a **lookout point** above. You'll be rewarded by spectacular views of a myriad of blues. From the right side of the hill there's access to a hiking trail leading down to **Marae Aehautai**. The location of this sacred site would have been chosen because of the awesome views of Mount Otemanu and way out, beyond the reef, to Taha'a and Raiatea on the horizon. Around this area there are other marae, plus more American guns that were strategically placed here during WWII.

Continuing along the road, after passing the bay you'll go by **Pension Bora Lagoonarium** on the lagoon side. When you see very marshy land with a row of simple homes, a church, and a couple of tiny stores, you're at **Anau Village**. On the water side you will see signs for **shuttle-boat bases** where Le Meridien, St Regis and the Four Seasons resorts pick up and put down guests and staff, to transfer them to and from the outer motus.

After reaching **Fitiiu Point** you'll observe a few houses and next you'll be at **Taimoo Bay**. Beyond this there are a few miles of coconut palm plantations and scuba land crabs interspersed by the occasional dwelling. Pushing onwards you will spot the **Marine Museum** which showcases models of famous ships that have visited Tahiti. Unfortunately, it's only open occasionally and has an admission fee.

As you approach **Point Taihi**, watch carefully to locate the steep walking track leading uphill to the World War II radar station on **Popoti Ridge**. From up there you have a bird's eye view across the lagoon to the airport motu.

Shortly after resuming your tour across the top of the island you'll be surprised by a group of **4 overwater bungalows and 11 mountainside apartments** on poles. They're holiday rentals available for visitors wanting to stay a week or more. Two are given a touch of glamor by being called **Marlon Brando's**, as he was their illustrious, past owner.

The **Pearl Beach Resort land base**, for accessing its private shuttle boat, is located at the point where you turn directly southwards along **Faanui Bay**. At this point an old **sea-plane ramp and shipping wharf**, constructed by the American Seabees stationed here, comes into view. If you look carefully up the hillside, above the concrete water tank, you can see one more **U.S. coastal gun** that was never fired. After passing the former marine base keep your eyes on the area between the road and the bay to locate the large stones of **Marae Fare-Opu**. Stop for a closer look at the interesting turtle petroglyphs inscribed on this ancient temple.

Ironically, the next building of interest is the **Protestant church**, at the head of the bay. The unpaved, **dirt road running inland**, beside the church, goes up to Parara Mountain Artist and later narrows into a winding walking track. Robust hikers can follow this path over the saddle of the ridge top, and cross the inner island, to arrive at Vairau Bay slightly south of Fitiiu Point. This is strictly a dry weather activity, as when it rains the rough terrain becomes slippery and dangerous. Even the experienced official guide won't traverse it without appropriate conditions.

Continuing around Faanui Bay to its west side, you will approach the **main shipping wharf,** which is also a legacy of the American base. This is where cargo vessels and inter-island ferries now arrive and dock.

Marae Marotetini comes into view just 100 meters westwards from the wharf. This royal temple was restored by Dr Yosihiko Sinoto in 1968. The chief families of Bora Bora are buried nearby.

Next you will arrive at the **Bora Bora Yacht Club** which had to be re-built after the 2010 cyclone. If you've time, go in for a fresh pina colada or a snack. High on the mountain side **two more American guns** still watch silently from between the tropical vegetation, strategically aimed towards the only entry pass through the lagoon's protective ring of coral.

Looking across the lagoon from this side of the island you will see the **Pearl Beach Resort** on **Motu Tevairoa** (to the right) and the closed (after the 2010 cyclone) **Bora Bora Lagoon Resort** on **Motu Toopua** (to the left). Tiny **Motu Tapu** is also in view, just past Motu Toopua. It's available to guests at the Hilton Nui, for private celebrations, and some tours utilize it for a motu stop. The Nui is out of sight, in seclusion, spread along an awesome white-sand beach, at the back of Toopua.

Just before you arrive back at Vaitape center, you'll go by Bathy's **Top Dive centre**, which is the biggest in Bora Bora, and peaceful **St Helen's shopping center,** at the side of the lagoon.

What to Pack for Tahiti

The following list of essentials is a result of years of discovering things we needed to have brought, after we were on an island, thousands of miles from regular shops. It includes specific items that are usually necessary for getting the most value from your Bora Bora vacation.

The Smarties Check List

- Swimsuits - three or four or more!
- Light 'throw over' sun shirts in white or soft colors (to prevent sunburn)
- Light weight clothing - sun dresses, skirts, tops, t-shirts, shorts
- Lightweight waterproof/windproof jacket
- Rash vest and board shorts
- Sun hat that folds up in your bag, can get wet, and won't blow off in wind
- Flip flops and comfy sandals
- Reef shoes
- Snorkel and fins
- Walking shoes - ONLY if you plan on hiking inland
- Waterproof sunscreen
- Insect repellant
- Underwater camera - a must if you intend snorkeling. This is essential to capture the awesome underwater world
- SLR camera - if you want the best pics of Bora Bora beaches, Mt Otemanu and other stunning scenery
- International power adapter
- Large supply of SD cards - you're going to the most beautiful island in the world!
- Waterproof day bag - for excursions or laying around the beach
- Some nice things to slip into for evening - not formal wear, just smart casual
- A special pair of sandals or shoes for evening - without heels, ladies

Made in the USA
Coppell, TX
25 March 2022

75527582R00070